Awakened by Destiny

"Positioned and Focused"

Shanae B. Govan

Awakened by Destiny:Positioned and Focused

Copyright © 2018 by Shanae Govan

All rights reserved. This book or any portion thereof may not be reproduced or used in any manner whatsoever without the express written permission of the publisher except for the use of brief quotations in a book review. Printed in the United States of America

First Printing
ISBN 978-1-943284-26-9 (pbk.)
ISBN 978-1-943284-27-6 (ebk)

A2Z Books Publishing
Lithonia, GA 30058
www.A2ZBooksPublishing.net
Manufactured in the United States of America
A2Z Books Publishing has allowed this work to remain exactly as the author intended, verbatim.

❖ *Table of Contents*

- ❖ Dedication 1
- ❖ Chapter 1:   *Dear Destiny* 5
- ❖ Chapter 2:   *The Journey* 11
  - ✓ EMBRACING the Journey 13
  - ✓ Deciding to Get Over It 24
  - ✓ Growing the RIGHT way 28
  - ✓ Shifting towards PURPOSE 35
- ❖ Chapter 3:   *The Process* 43
  - ✓ Evolving during the PROCESS 45
  - ✓ Waiting While HE Works 49
  - ✓ Building Your FAITH 60
- ❖ Chapter 4: *The Middle* 72
  - ✓ TRAILBLAZING towards Victory 73
  - ✓ Living through the Defeated MOMENT 81
  - ✓ Advancing BEYOND the Comfortable Place 95
- ❖ Chapter 5: *The Destination* 110
  - ✓ Dividing the ASSETS from liabilities 112
  - ✓ ENDURING a Tough Loss 124
  - ✓ Transitioning in Your NOW 128

❖ DEDICATION

Dear Self,

There shall not be lived another day weighted in captivity of what has been wrongfully done to you over the course of time. You shall not forfeit your rightful place in Victory. You are not to be victimized by the broken promises, defeat, hopelessness or the emotional rollercoaster. No longer will you choose to settle for less than what you purposefully deserve, which is your birthright. Not another day will you walk in shame or guilt from the past mistakes that you have selflessly chosen out of obligation to something that has held you captive in the mental state of your mind. Today, you have the right to choose freedom; liberty is here to deliver you from every weighted chain that has been attached to your dark thoughts. These thoughts that have infused insecurities, low self-esteem, depression, oppression, suppression, anger, bitterness, rejection, defeat, hate, jealousy, and sorrow. The tears you have cried hopelessly are finally at their designated point of, "NO MORE". This is the day that has come to rid you of the heartache of harboring despair and abandonment by the ones who vowed to never leave, the loved ones who walked away and intentionally watched as you suffered at the foot of their disappointments, the friends who purposefully betrayed your trust, the toxic relationship that left you longing for acceptance. At last, your breakthrough has come. This is it. You have made your arrival to the place called DESTINY. Pick up your bags of hope, joy, promise, love, wholeness, and forgiveness. The journey awaits your arrival.

Sincerely,

Someone who's been Awakened by Destiny

I want to extend the assurance that I am just like you. I am not a professional scholar; nor am I an evangelical minister traveling around the country. I am no clinical psychologist or perfectionists at life. I am simply someone just like you. I'm a believer who is striving to endure adversity in this world. I am in the trenches with you and as you are, I'm trying to stay afloat. My mission is to find a way to align with my destiny. It is with great hope and expectation that after you read this heartfelt message delivered through me, by the Hands of GOD that you're able to understand why you had to go through the way you did, in order to get to this beautiful place called DESTINY…

-Let's Go

❖ Chapter 1:
Dear Destiny

"Hold fast to dreams for if dreams die
Life is a broken-winged that cannot fly.
Hold fast to dreams for when dreams go
Life is a barren field frozen with snow"
-Langston Hughes

I am no longer lifeless or asleep while anticipating for the next alarm to sound for me to awake. I am now my own self-motivated alarm clock. I have vanished from allowing life to by-pass because of my failures or mistakes. But now, I am awakened by my future. I am now pressing beyond the higher calling **"My Purpose"**. I discovered that there exists purpose in adversity, but now I have positioned myself to attain something greater, *"My Destiny"*. This road is not undemanding; there are several detours, bumps, and bruises along the way. Many afflictions are attached to this adjacent cycle of life, but if endured, the glory to be revealed in the end will be worth the tears. The frustration, the pain and discomfort, being broken, forsaken, and tossed aside have come to a permanent halt because they are no longer a part of where God is preparing to advance you to.

What is *destiny*? It is the venue where purpose has been birthed and your future awaits you with esteemed expectation; the place that positions believers to embody a stance of victory. You have now shifted to a space in your life of being an overcomer and more than a conqueror. Many of you may be wondering, what does that look like? How do I know that I have pressed into my destiny? It very well may not look the same for each individual but its intent signifies an equal platform for everyone. *Destiny* was designed for you to evolve into being the best version of yourself and the only way you can get to this phase of your life is by accepting and embracing the difficulties that life offers. Avail yourself of the hardships; they only come to prepare you for what is ahead. You must not negate what is trying to awaken on the inside of your inner being.

We all have a byway to *destiny*. Whether we take it or not is another question, but there is surely undeniable access to it. The loaded and intensified pressure births out our new beginning. Diamonds are developed in the lowest part of the earth under the most difficult circumstances. They must undergo a process of being constrained and withstand heated intensity before they can come forth as a most appreciated rare gem on Earth. Just as diamonds, after gold has been proved through the fire, then it comes out well-developed as the most valuable and prized possession. The only way the next level of your potential can come into prominence is by growing through maturity, pains, learning to be propelled by life's circumstances, and embracing the challenges of being pursued by what has need of you. God has a plan that specifically has included you in it. There is KINGDOM business that anticipates your arrival. The seasonal and well-timed winds of purpose and favor are beckoning for your acceptance but it is up to you to seize and take hold of the keys to your future.

Shanae B. Govan

Most of us like to think of destiny as a position of radiant or angelic scenery, that comes without distress or misfortune. I have grown to learn that the gateway to destiny is *monstrous*. Only the strong and defended can endure the tests of adversity to persevere on this journey. At the point of wanting to throw in the towel and turn around, we must abandon what things look like in the natural and put on our spiritual eyesight before realizing we are closer to our daybreak than ever before. This is not the time to call it quits, or to take a break. We must shift to our second gear whenever we feel as if we want to give up. Take on the mindset of trusting the process while enjoying the journey of being approved by the tests of life. We should comprehend that true winners never quit, and quitters never win. Your alternative gear should not allow you to forfeit your rights by waving the white flag out of frustration when running this race. Instead, it presses you to pick up your word and apply it to your situation. There is something that has been embedded on the inside of each of us that will help us kick to our next shift when faced with opposition. Life is set up that way. We must accelerate to our second gear when our backs are against the wall. I've found myself in situations as such, and have watched

God become the wall for me to lean against showing that He's my strength and that I don't have to stand alone.

The succeeding winds of being an overcomer echo *"I am victorious, I will not quit, I can do this, and I will not give up because God has me in his plans."* This indicated restful place is like a life-line that says you've come too far and invested too much to throw in the towel now. You must go after that college degree, pursue that new career, start that new business, rededicate your life to God, start that diet, and rebuild your confidence and self-esteem. Second gear propels you closer to destiny; it does not hold you back. It says that come what may, I am choosing to stand in faith and I trust that I am stronger than what I am currently up against.

The promise cannot deny you of what has already been given to you as a birthright. What is the promise? **Jeremiah 29:11 says "For I know the plans that I have for you declares the Lord, plans to prosper you and not harm you, to give you a hope and a future".** Because of this affirmation by God, you have no other choice but to step into *destiny*; there is no possible way that you can forfeit this fight. It has already been fought and won for you. Although the road to your future will birth distressing times, lonely days, frustrated moments, and misunderstanding of your purpose at times, you cannot forget what His word has declared. It will not harm you, but prosper you. There is surely a good hope and future even through the heartache, the anguish, and adversity that will come.

Destiny was not designed to be easily attained, but the treasures that wait thereafter once you have been proved and tested through the fire, cannot be fathomed. I believe that anything worth having is attached to work, sacrifice, despair, and discomfort; but it only arises in our lives to create a life-changing testimony for others to see. We first must embrace the process.

"Challenges are what make life interesting and overcoming them is what makes life meaningful"

-Joshua J. Marine

❖ Chapter 2:

The Journey

"Have I not commanded you, be strong and courageous do not be afraid; do not be discouraged, for the Lord your God will be with you wherever you go"

–Joshua 1:9 (NIT)

The journey is often devalued because of the process it takes to get to it. We should not be in such a speeded race to get to our destination, but instead just delight in the orchestrated steps on the journey. God systematically has set our lives up to coincide with a necessary course to overcome life's circumstances, but we must first learn to embody the pathway of where we are headed.

Everyone's path does not look the same. We all are not going towards the same goals, nevertheless, we are convinced to take the appropriate steps to get to our placement toward favoring our target.

This is the place where you can discover what you are made of. Anyone can feel secure when you are surrounded by people who support what you are doing, but how do you respond when you are abandoned and left to figure it out on your own? The journey is beautiful in its own way. The pursuit is not given to the swift nor is the battle to the strong but to those who endure to the end. This is what we were told in the book of Ecclesiastes. Therefore, our pace should mirror making the decision to take a position and enjoy the ride. Embody being broken, left out, forgotten, hopeless, and shame. It all has been appropriately designed to make you stronger for what lies ahead on this systematic path by the King of Kings. Own where you are headed.

✓ EMBRACING the Journey

"But those who hope in the Lord will renew their strength. They will soar on wings like eagles; they will run and not grow weary, they will walk and not be faint"

–Isaiah 40:31 (NIV)

Have you ever felt as if life was so difficult and the only option you had was to run away to gain a new start? Ever felt as if the life you were given was unfair or unfortunate and you desired to live in someone else's shoes? Or maybe you have been in a place or season where it seemed as if everything and everyone was against you and the only other option you had was to stand alone and disassociate yourself from everyone because you felt misunderstood? How about thinking to yourself that if only *"this"* was different or if only *"that"* would not have been done or said, then I would not be in this position in my life right now? What about just having the desire to lay in bed all day, cry yourself to sleep with hopes that when you wake up everything about your life would disappear or change from what had initially happened or been done? Anyone ever have these thoughts surface in your mind besides me?

The truth of the matter is; we all have experienced some type of undeserved actions that have been intentionally or unintentionally done to us over the course of time. Life was not designed to be problem-free or without issues. Those experiences that we have faced in our lives help bring us to a designated place of growth and sobriety if we allow them to serve their rightful purpose. Once we decide to commit to the shift in our thinking and gravitate towards the truth of our issues, then it propels us to another dimension in moving towards *destiny*. This concept is often difficult for us to do but it is so necessary. It is imperative to grasp this remedy to secure our seat in victory; and honestly, that is exactly what you must do to matriculate on this journey. Some of you may ask, well why is that?

Why do you have to be the bigger person and choose to forgive someone who has purposefully hurt you? Or why should you let go of the rejection caused by the ones you needed most? Is it even possible to move on with your life and press towards your future as if the past had never happened? What can you do to go on to the next chapter of your story while leaving all the negative aspects thereof behind? What should you do to bury the past and commit to beckoning towards a new tomorrow? Why must you leave that life behind and abandon that way of thinking? How do you disconnect yourself from the one person who you depended on most? Why is it that you cannot harbor those feelings of defeat or insecurities any longer? Is it possible to even move forward without ceasing? I am so glad you asked…

Destiny can never fit into a comfort zone. This journey was not designed to supply individuals with a pacifier or with a blanket for the cold and lonely nights. This road is not easy, but it is worth the glory that will be revealed at the end of the tunnel but only through abandoning your old habits and way of thinking that has robbed you of your future. This place has no room for quitters or people that will question the route of where God is taking them and not trust His master plan. The set and appropriate time has come to shift us to our second gear. It is past the time to kick and maneuver through the adversity sent to detour you. Forfeiting is not an available option on this journey. You must not give up or give in during this fight out of fear of failing. There is no failure in God, therefore, losing out is not a part of this process.

The evolution of time is groomed and carved by Gifted Hands. God is the potter who brings together the unstructured pieces, and our broken lives are the clay that He uses to patch those things back into their rightful place creating a masterpiece shaped in His image. Although life's storms may appear to be outweighed in number, He has already strategically placed each of us in our designated assignment on earth. We should realize and know that the most beautiful piece of this journey of being sensitively crafted and molded through the process towards *destiny* is the most delicate piece of the puzzle. The necessary grooming phase that we all must go through, births out in us what we will desperately need to secure our survival. He is not always within arm's reach, or visible. There will come times where along this hard, dark, irritating, lonely, and frustrating place we will become blinded intentionally by our situations and the deep waves of life to increase our level of faith. Growth is uncomfortable but necessary.

The dark room, the low place, the isolated position is where the most beautiful masterpieces of life are developed; and once the light is deemed on the project after it has gone through the proper and necessary process of being strategically customized, then you can see from an abstract level of appreciation. These moments of trials and tribulations specifically force your faith to be tried through adversity, and if you choose to stand in faith and faint not, it is then that God will do exceedingly and abundantly above all that we can ask or think according to the power that works within us; but we must first make the commitment within ourselves to stick it out. You must embrace and embody the process.

This position is congruent to growth. It also crossed over into my world of work as a young coach while in Mississippi. There were so many issues attached to my job other than the common responsibilities. Along with this position came the pressures of being the first African American teacher and coach in the school's history in forty-four long years of predominately one race which was not mine in a racially divided town in the Mississippi Delta. With that blueprint alone, I had to realize that every day when I showed up to work, I represented more than just myself. Day by day, when I arrived at the parking lot, I symbolized history and change. And this seat was specifically laced with the restored and renewed mindset about a culture of people who were once prejudged to be uneducated, country, low class, and ghetto.

God strategically positioned me to sit in a seat that unmasked my race and culture. I then had to accept that character and integrity were my focal points when arriving at work and that even during adversity, I had to commit myself to those moral and ethical standards. Although at times, I may have felt mistreated because of my age, gender, or race. In those moments, it was bigger than me, but it had everything to do with a legacy that would later be formed in a dying community and would now bring hope, change, love, and sobriety.

Now, two separate races could come together at basketball games and watch a zealous, driven, ambitious, and motivated young rookie coach mentor, push, and uplift her players. Although I had to endure some of the toughest situations of my life that at times overwhelmed me, I had to understand that it was all for a greater purpose than what my natural eyes could see. One incident changed my life forever. It was after a player had smarted off to me and cussed after I asked a question, I sent her to the locker room during our game. Her father was very angry and upset and while the game was going on, he decided to come question my call on sending his daughter to the locker room.

Initially, as he approached me while coaching on the sideline, I ignored him and kept my composure. He ended up making one racial remark as he asked why would I do something so ignorant as to sending his daughter to the locker room because he felt as if she was the best player. He ignored the fact that she had disrespected me which caused me to put her in the position that she was in and immediately blamed me for her actions. At that moment, I had two options. One, I could ignore him and continue coaching or two, I could step outside of my character as he did and retaliate with derogatory words.

It was in that instant that I knew I was being tested; not by the man, but by the growing path towards my destiny. I had to understand that again, that moment had nothing to do with me, but it had everything to do with where I was headed, my character and integrity. My girls were on the bench modeling my behavior and watching my every move, even my body language. Although I was fighting back the tears during this abandoned and isolated moment because of the embarrassment for one, and the fact that no one stood up for me, I calmly kept coaching and shifted my focus on my girls because they were most important at the time.

After the game, my girls were so quiet in the locker room. One of my sophomores who I had admired so much stepped up and made the comment that I was her hero and that she hated that I had to go through that during the game. I smiled and told her that my shoes are tough to fill and that God knew exactly what He was doing when He placed me in this position. I made the comment to my players that honorableness will take you wherever you want to go. Although they will never understand what I felt, in a room full of people who were not of my race and being insulted and disrespected by an angry parent without being supported by anyone in the gym. That moment of my life taught me so much and I gained many life lessons from it. At twenty-four years old at the time, I can honestly say that I embraced wisdom from that incident which will stick with me for the rest of my life.

God was building me for the day where I could stand and testify as a change agent, someone who had embarked on foreign territory in an exiled land but for His glory. For his set purpose that He could get the honor out of it all; and to think that one of the greatest opportunities of my life would be attached to so much affliction and heartache. The good days outweighed the bad by a million, but of those days where I wanted to lose hope or felt all alone, I can naturally say that God was my anchor and He put people in place to be my hope and true friends.

People like Mrs. Jennifer Joyner; someone who did not see race, but as Dr. Martin Luther King Jr. stated in his *"I have a Dream"* speech, she judged me by the content of my character. That lady was my backbone those three years in the rural Mississippi Delta. God knew that I would need someone who could understand my processes and trust with my fears at times when I felt as if I was on an island by myself. She not only appreciated me for what I did for her two girls as my players on the basketball team, but she loved me for my heart and desire to do the right thing even when at times I was unjustifiably treated.

I believe that what defines true growth is when you choose to treat others well despite being misused or talked about. Again, it was never about me from the beginning when God planted me there, but it had everything to do with a culture of people who needed someone to be their voice because they had become silenced; someone who stood as an advocate because they were blinded by race. Although my time expired quickly in MS, after three years, I can admit that not only did I leave as a better coach, professional, and friend; but I left as a better person and it was all because I made the decision to commit to the journey of accepting adversity.

Often, God keeps us in seasons so we can get the lessons that we need to advance. We become frustrated and stagnated out of not wanting to be challenged and flourish in areas where we have become comfortable. As a result of embracing this concept, I became a more valuable asset to the society, developed a greater sense of character, and could effectively lead my girls not just as a coach, but also as a mentor. Embrace the journey of evolving the right way, instead of rushing your process of getting to destiny. We cannot afford to skip levels of production because the result will always come back not complete.

Everyone has become aggravated and annoyed with the manner of waiting. It is simple for God to perform the promise that He has spoken concerning our situation, but the complexity of it comes when God is trying to develop us into who we need to be to inherit the promise. The process is at times held up because it takes longer for God to get us ready to be the person He needs us to be so we will not destroy what He has for us. Prematurely, if we were to inherit what has been set aside before time and before we are ready, then inevitably, we will devalue, misuse, and abuse it. God is just not about giving us what we want, but His objective is complete and precise. We must be groomed and go through the necessary measure of having all that has been prepared for us. Embrace the journey.

✦ *My prayer as you learn to embrace the Journey*

God, I thank you for teaching us to trust your plans even when we do not always understand your methods. Lead us to a place of peace and rest in understanding that you are the author and finisher of our faith. I thank you because I know that through you, our journey will be fulfilled to its greatest potential. Even in the darkest hour of our lives, I thank you because I believe that we can find hope and assurance in knowing that your word is a lamp unto our feet and a light unto our path. Because you are our anchor, it is impossible for us to sink under life's circumstances. We trust you with the plans you have for our lives. Thank you for allowing destiny to awaken in us. Amen.

✓ *Deciding to Get Over It*

"Forget what happened in the past, and do not dwell on events from long ago"

–Isaiah 43:18 (GWT)

In my twenty-five years of a short-lived life, I have grown to discover that there are some issues we must "get over" before we can advance in God and get to where He is beckoning us to. Each of us, have endured difficult trials that should have taken us out. Many of us, if we could, we would have bailed out of our purpose, but there was an awakening in the pit of your belly that whispered: "you can't die here". I have been mishandled by loved ones, by friends who vowed to stand by my side, a church family that I worshiped with Sunday after Sunday, and more. But it was in those moments that I learned to sustain myself and evolved into the knowledge and true essence of "moving forward".

I have examined it to be much effortless to waste essential time sitting in bitterness, instead of pressing on towards forgiveness. Honestly, there are some circumstances and people that we should just learn to overlook if we must aspire to get to the sweet place called *Destiny*. Growing up, I was informed that certain people are assigned to our lives just to deliver frustration to our situation. They are often referred to as roadblocks, curveballs, or in better terms, *"haters"*. Don't you know that it is those kinds of people who help thrush you to the destination? They envy what is on the inside of you because there is an admiration and infatuation for them to have it also, but they do not understand what it takes to inherit what you have been blessed with. It is so essential that we realize the value in *"getting over it"*. There is an exceeding amount of life to be lived than to be derailed by those that don't like you or who have mistreated you.

What has positioned me to acquire a deeper level of understanding when battling with this issue is remembering what Jesus had to endure by His own people. It was not the nonbelievers who persecuted Him, but it was those that walked with Him; Judas. Sometimes, the ones who you hold close and believe have your best interest at heart, are those who in the end, turn and betray you. But just as Jesus forgave Judas, we must do the same. He knew that His assignment was greater than the treason of one of His disciples. In all actuality, that is what inspired the equality of passion for people and the true understanding of Grace. It says that we don't deserve it, but God grants it anyway. This is the mindset we must have while striving to move past the hurt, abandonment, and lies. Those situations had to occur so that you and I could advance to another place in the fulfillment of who we are destined to be.

Dismantle that sense of entitlement. Truly, it is actually one of the extensive components that set us back from moving on. No one owes us anything. We have not been so great, or so good that we did not deserve what happened. There comes a time where you disengage from the shackles of being a victim and realize that you are much stronger than what transpired or what was said about you. That is where the enemy tries to bind us in stagnation. He wants us to live in those falsities, believing those things that have no truth and serve no purpose. But you must first, have the appetite to overcome it. It is necessary that even in this walk; we do not allow people to detain us in bondage of the past. One of my favorite sayings is, *"misery loves company"*. It is so prevalent and true. You cannot afford to waste energy and effort on those problems. It serves us nothing to live under those matters of life. Commit to moving on.

Mishaps occur in our lives that bombard where we are and knock us off our feet. God knows what we have the strength to endure, and those situations that we cannot tackle on our own, He has the power to clear them out of the way enabling us to continue to embark on the journey that awaits us with great expectation. Therefore, it is so vital that we remain anchored in Him. He stabilizes us and gives us all the necessary and prominent tools needed to get over the issues that have transpired in our lives having the will to take us out. Be thankful for His continued mercy that delivers us out of all the afflictions. Trials bring strength and wholeness to the things that look hopeless. The truth of the matter is, it is not that we have not wanted to throw in the towel, or walk away but it has always been the purpose that He put on the inside of our inner being that keeps us pressing forward. We must know that we are more than our current condition. This state of our situation does not dictate the destination. It is just a passing through terminal that we must bypass to get to where God wants to advance us to. Rejection brings about humility and meekness. Those valley moments when you feel left out and mistreated push you closer to the foot of the Cross and develop a greater sense of quality and security in who He is in our lives. Embrace the Adversity.

✓ *Growing the RIGHT way*

"Don't just grow good, grow RIGHT"

- Omega George

When we don't grow on our own, life will give us the opportunity to develop through a necessary crisis to prepare us for where we are headed. *Destiny* is a place of continuous, constant, and progressive seasons. Our matriculation to the next phase therefore depends on growing the right way. Many times, in life, we become stagnated in our approach to advance towards our future. Certain circumstances present themselves as opportunities to help us mature to maximize our potential for the future glory. Because this mechanism is often mishandled and devalued, we miss out on flourishing properly which prevents us from becoming the best version of ourselves in order to secure our survival on the next level of purpose. Seemingly in life, we all have repeated cycles time after time because we choose to remain at a standstill and become complacent. Instead of growing good, grow right.

This practice looks different for everyone. The main concept that we must understand when it has to do with properly sealing our advancement is dismantling the high level of pride while becoming groomed to reign in this coming seat. Rushing does not benefit you in this area; it does not reflect growing right. Good enough will not be sufficient in this component of maturing because it will even run its course one day, which will result in you having to repeat the same course over again. That is why it is imperative that while you can, get the lesson at its appropriate time to develop the right way even if it means that you must take a backseat to some things or people. I would much rather humble myself right now and be able to move forward, than have issues with pride and stubbornness which will result in a delayed journey.

It is not in our power to decide which areas we will properly cultivate right in and which we will not. Holistically, we all should learn to encompass this procedure so that we can walk in wholeness. Regardless of how big or small the issue is, you must choose to acquire this standard in all aspects thereof. Whether it be for relationships, occupations, friendships, or personal development, it is indeed necessary and vital.

My struggle began with failing to ask for help, although I knew that I needed it. God had to dismantle that selfish part of my character to get me to where he was trying to elevate my life. Had I not been forced by uncomfortable situations and evolved and accepted that I was required to change this deadly pattern and way of thinking, I would have surrendered all my rights to destiny. Nothing was worth it, so I was compelled to let it go. I had to consciously commit to yielding to the transition of growth. I eventually matured to the place in my life where I decided that I craved for God more than anything else; I reflected Him.

Nevertheless, I had to rid myself of pride, selfishness, and hypocrisy if I wanted to excel the right way.

The key to wholeness is acceptance of your truth. We should first own our truth. No longer did I choose to operate in this unbeneficial pattern because it only prolonged the gateway to *destiny*. We will never be able to advance in the Kingdom of God by entertaining these measures in our frame of mind; they hold us back. For a long time, I was blinded to my issues, but then, there came a day where I was awakened by something greater. Nevertheless, since then, I have not turned or had the appetite to go back. I encompassed the desire to be all that God wanted me to be in and through Him, and it modeled change. It echoed truth. I began to speak His truths concerning my life while detoxing from every lie that I thought was essential to get to the next level. We do not have to manipulate situations to proceed to our higher calling. When God makes a way that sums it all up, nothing can stop His plans or get in the track of what He has for your life; the only thing that can is you. I removed myself and allowed God to have His way. I embraced the journey.

Life has a clever approach of either forcing you to grow up or it will outpace you. I gravitated to a matured state in mind that I was not going to allow this delicate moment in time to leave me out. We must understand that some issues are significantly bigger than we are. Everything that transpires in our lives is to help us overcome and see from another place; no longer being victims, but instead victors! When growing the right way, you must embrace each stage of the developmental process. Some seasons last longer, some lessons are tougher than others, but they all hold their own significant placement. Obtaining a connection to the right people in this phase of our lives is detrimental to our survival. I lost several friendships but I gained more valuable ones that were tied to my destination. It is important that we do not carry seasonal people along the journey with us; it only clusters our judgment and thought process. Some may not all the time have the ability to see the vision that we are seeking to birth out. Losing people along the voyage is necessary, therefore, you must figure out who is worth going to destiny with you, and who is not.

There came a desperate moment in time where I did not allow the past to haunt me or walk in defeat because of the countless effortless mistakes that I had once made, the failed relationships, and the disappointments caused by the ones I loved the most. I had to choose to press past it all. *Destiny* awaited my arrival. God thought enough of me to place people in my life that represented accountability. Initially, I had to mature and develop to the place where I took ownership of being my best friend, motivator, and push element. I could not wait on others to pat me on the back and say, you've got this, it will be okay, don't worry about it, it will get better; but I had to tell myself those things and keep pushing it. There comes a deciding shift in your life where you advance to the position to let people be people. We recognize the fact that life is going to let you down, but you must not be detoured by the current, instead, find your anchor in God. That is exactly what I did during this phase of my life. I valued who God had placed around me at the time and moved with the cloud of growing the right way.

Excelling has a peculiar way of forcing you to forfeit compromising to satisfy the needs of others. This realm pushes you to adjust in making conscious decisions that lead to self-pleasure. I learned the difference between growing good and growing right. When individuals who are connected to you, no longer help but begin to prohibit you from prospering to the maximum capacity of who you were designed to be, then that is the sign that reevaluation should take place. When you expect people to fill a void that only can be filled by God, you will forever be empty. You must not allow your life to become tied down to people who cannot launch or help advance you into your future; they will only pull you back. It is important that we release, and leap forward towards our greater calling; *Destiny*.

Finally, I had arrived at a consistent place in my life. I did not allow myself to become entangled with the inconsistencies of becoming overwhelmed or weighed down by the actions or choices of others. When I made the conscious decision to flourish forward in that area of my life, it was as if I had excelled towards something greater that was necessary for where I was headed. My spiritual father, Apostle Isaac Jenkins, played a significant role in helping me grasp this concept. He helped teach me effective strategies to win the battle of emotional issues that I struggled with within myself concerning my self-esteem, confidence, ability to grow past what people had sculpted me to believe about my past, and a host of other issues. Mr. Isaac was a great influential piece of the puzzle during this stage of my life; He was consistent and this helped me go through the grooming process in order to become who God had designed me to be.

✓ *Shifting towards PURPOSE*

"Above all else, guard your heart, for everything you do flows from it"

-Proverbs 4:23(NKJV)

We all know what happens when a shift takes places; it propels you one way or the other. It is my hope that we all desire a positive exchange to take course in our lives so that we can advance in reaching the main goal; arrival to *Destiny*. One of my favorite verses in the Bible is found in the book of Jeremiah chapter 29:11, it reassures us that regardless of what comes, God has a greater purpose that He has already configured and mapped out for you. There are no stipulations attached to this word. What happened to you is not of any significance, God said, it was not fit to harm you, but instead to prosper you. This is where the change in our thinking should kick in. We must train our minds to believe and not waiver from this promise that He has made. Shift your thinking.

The battle of the mind is one of the most delicate forces that the enemy uses to detour, distract, discourage, and defeat us as people of God. It is his skillful tactic to paint us a dysfunctional picture of our past and to bind us there. This keeps us from transitioning forward. Our thoughts should pattern and align with where we are headed. Harboring guilt, shame, bitterness, or depression in the cortex of our thinking prohibits the shift. Each of us must decide to elevate our way of thinking and refute the mental strategy of the enemy so that we do not embody his way of blinding us from what God has set out for us to attain. We must be strong-minded. Shift your thinking.

This was a significant area that I battled with while adjusting my thinking concerning several areas of my life. That was the toughest issue that I dealt with during the process of embracing the journey. I would allow the way things looked or appeared to distract me. That is not faith. Hebrews 11:1 states, *"**Now faith is the substance of things hoped for and the evidence of things not seen**".* Nevertheless, we know that life is not about what things look like in the natural, but it is based on the things hoped for; the unseen. If you can see it, then you do not need faith. The effort to believe past what I saw was so strong that I would forfeit myself from reaching my fullest potential even in my walk with God because of my unbelief when things seemed to be turning for the worst. His word says, without faith it is impossible to please Him. I had to come to a place that no matter what came in my life, regardless of what it appeared to be or how difficult it was for me to believe that He was going to make a way; I had to choose to rest in faith. My belief system was all I had. That is the place where God wants us. When He has us in a position where we have nothing to hold onto besides our faith, then He can get the total glory from our situations. But we must first, shift our thinking.

When modifying your thinking, another key component is being mindful of whom you are connected to. It all goes back to embracing the idea of letting go. Although it is complicated and sometimes uncomfortable, we must make the necessary changes in this area of our lives to protect the arrival to *Destiny*. When an exchange or shift takes place, sometimes individuals are removed from their position and often it is a result of not being anchored or in a position of stability. I began to learn to never allow people to make me feel bad because I elevated my thinking, and repositioned my focus to having the desire to become more in life. Advancement pushes us to surround ourselves with like-minded vessels; it only helps the transition go smoother.

It is important that in this realm of processing through that we reconstruct our strategies of how we intake information. We can no longer allow certain things to confuse our way of breaking down situations. Negative thoughts cannot dwell in our mental state of thinking. They do not give us benefits to what God has for us. You must alter and elevate the way you conceive information. My friend would often call it, learning to compartmentalize. Do not allow your emotions to dictate how you choose to believe or feel. Emotions are only temporary that is why it is vital that we do not react based on emotions. Consequently, before I grew to the place where I lived intentionally in the moment of faith, I had the difficulty of learning to adjust my way of strategizing whenever I would become emotionally drained with situations. I had to mature in this area of my life and not be like the waves whenever things came my way to detour me from the promises of God.

Our mental state is probably the most valuable possession that we have when it comes to making decisions and being cognitively aware of what lies ahead of us. If we are not careful with what we allow to go on in our minds, whether it be words, music, or anything toxic, we will struggle with the mindset. The way you perceive situations is all a mindset. It reflects who you are. It is important that we elevate our way of strategizing no matter what we have experienced while growing up or what we have seen in the past or may be currently facing. We must stick to the promises of God and believe what His word says. Do not give the enemy any room to operate in your mind and torment you with how things look or what has happened in the past.

Purpose has a plan greater than what you naturally can see. Shifting towards your future calls for you to become mentally stable in knowing and training your thoughts not to waiver in the face of difficult situations and circumstances. God promised that He would never put more on us than we can bear. Whenever negative thoughts arise, you must feed them with the word of God. This is the only remedy for getting through these moments of frustration that have come to rob you of your future and destiny. We must starve those doubts and feed our thoughts with the truth. God's word is what should replace the lies of the enemy and the limitless insecurities that try to overtake our minds. Faith and worry cannot dwell in the same place. Remember, belief is not congruent to what makes sense or what we can see in the natural, God's ways are higher than ours and His thoughts are also. It does not matter if it make sense to you or not, it is not up to us to try and figure it out; if God said it, then you must train your mind to believe how He believes and choose to stand in faith. Shift your thinking.

At this point in my life, God had begun to open doors for me to travel and speak to young people all over the place. I can remember one night; the enemy had awakened me with the fear of not being an effective speaker. The thoughts of "not getting their attention, being boring, losing their interest, and being a hypocrite" all were imputed by him one night. I tossed and turned and even began to cry out to God because of these negative thoughts that the enemy had spoken to my mind. And then, I had to muscle up the strength to denounce those lies; because that is all the enemy can approach us with — a lie. There is no truth in him. No matter what he says or tries to use against you to get you off course, or question the route of where God is taking you, do not give him any authority over your mindset or thought pattern.

I know that God mandated me to this place in ministry and that He was going to perfect every work concerning me, and so did the enemy. That is why he battled me within my mind because he knew what God was getting ready to do in my life and where I was headed. His tactic was to try and discourage my dreams and throw me off course. We must all remain mentally tough when processing anything the enemy says to us. Remember, he is not qualified to approach us with the truth. Nothing he says is true or can go against the will of God. Therefore, you do not owe it to your emotions to get beat up by something he has said. Shift your thinking.

When your purpose in life is great, your cognitive processing should reflect where you are headed. Small-minded people can only think as far as their life is going to take them. Those of us whom God has ordained to live a purposeful life must take on the mindset of a champion. Come what may, do not allow yourself to be mentally stuck in a place where you do not belong. Do not stay up all night worrying yourself about what is going to happen; we serve a God who does not sleep or slumber, therefore, we should not try and handle situations that are greater than we are. It only wears us down in our thought process; it is another strategy of the enemy. It is the will of God that all our needs are supplied because we are important to Him. He told us in Proverbs 3:5-6 ***"Trust in the Lord with all your heart. Lean not unto your own understanding but in all your ways acknowledge Him and He will direct your path"***

❖ Chapter 3:

The Process

"For there is a proper time and procedure for every matter, though a person may be weighed down by trouble"

–Ecclesiastes 6:8 (NLT)

What develops when you skip a portion of the baking instructions in the course of making a pound cake? Will your dessert come out the way it should if you had followed the necessary routine steps it took to get the desired outcome? The process is probably the most avoided component in life that we negate when getting to our destination. Each level of growth has an important stage of development that it must go through before we can get to where we are headed. It is unavoidable and we must encompass and embrace this state of our being regardless of the difficulty it may seem to understand and blossom.

Processes are never simple, especially when growth is attached to it. Change is uncomfortable but it is vital to secure our placement in destiny. The only way that any of us will appreciate the evolution of becoming the best candidate for our ticket to the destination is by enduring the birthing pains while maturing through the process. The easiest thing to do in this phase of advancement is to give up and not allow life's pressures to push you in faith, stability, and trust in your belief system. The hard part comes by choosing to stick it out and press through those emotional scars and wounds to develop in you all the assets needed to reign in victory.

To everything that we go through in life, there is a season and a time as stated in Ecclesiastes 3:1. When the appropriate time has come, and we decide to endure being pressed and enjoy the journey, it allows the ride to the end to be smooth sailing. It is important not to lose sight because of delays and detours sent to discourage you. Sometimes, we all may have to experience a delayed journey, but the beauty in that is knowing that God will always see you through, just if you can stand the pull through the process.

✓ *Evolving during the PROCESS*

"We delight in the beauty of the butterfly, but rarely admit the changes it has gone through to achieve that beauty." -Maya Angelo

It becomes natural to negate the process of evolving through the proper stages to stay on the path towards your unborn future. Often, we become so distracted and overwhelmed with getting to our resting place, that we forget that the real appreciation is found during the actual steps to get there. Life strategically has been aligned by God to develop in us all the prominent tools that we will need to matriculate in each phase of the growth process. The summary of this level of maturity allows individuals to see the fruits of their labor and view it from a place of acceptance when we choose to pace through this stage, instead of rushing it.

Growth is a constant change that is necessary for our protection. Have you ever found yourself saying "I wish they would hurry up with our food?" What if the chef rushed through the process of properly preparing your meal and brought it out to you before it was time? Then would you find yourself satisfied with the result or would you be in a place of frustration? Something as simple as that analogy could help each of us put things in perspective as it relates to taking each step of this phase of our lives at the right pace and time. None of us want premature results, but often, we provide ourselves these outcomes because we all like things to be done at a fast pace; rather than sitting back and waiting in patience.

I was fortunate to move back home, and accept the head coaching job at my old high school. Both teams, Jr. and Sr. high had not had successful seasons in a few years. I previously had come from a similar situation when I coached in Mississippi. Nevertheless, just as I grew to accept that concept of developing in my players what they needed to become effective ballplayers, I had to take on the same mindset in this new position. It was a different team and environment, but the same method.

I had to tackle the journey, and now enjoy the mechanism of watching them elevate to the place that my former players had to get to so we could reach the destination. My focus was not on wins or loses; that would take care of itself. I had to shift my thinking and realize what was most important. And at that time, the most relevant element was to teach them about character, integrity, ambition and a work ethic. My goal was to administer the truth to them concerning the importance of not giving up when adversity shows up in our lives. They had become conditioned to giving in whenever things got tough, but here again, I found myself teaching those girls about the same principles that helped me endure some of the toughest challenges in my life. If we learned those concepts and developed in those areas, which would help us not only be sufficient athletes, but also productive adults, then the game of basketball would be easy. But we first had to commit to the process and realize it was a day-to-day grind. It was worth it.

In between shopping in town, I would often run into local people in the community, and the first thing they loved to ask was "is your team going to be good this year?" I would always smile and answer with "it's a process". And that was the truth. My girls had been so used to being morally and emotionally beat down with defeat that I would have to constantly build them up in the small areas just so that they would understand that life is hard; it will birth some of the most undesirable lessons but it is all worth it. Our focus became so engulfed with having good attitudes and pulling up one another that we eventually grew to the place where we could embody whatever came with being a Lady Eagle. Practices were hard. They were intense; but it made us. Just as I had to adjust, my girls had to also. They knew that although I was tough and stern, that I cared about them and it went above trying to get them to prove something to the community, it had everything to do with them committing to the process of life. It was much bigger than just a game. God wanted me to use basketball as the platform for something greater.

Just as this strategy of developing my players became a life lesson to me, it also coincided with my leadership role in ministry. Often, young girls and boys would reach out asking, "How did you become so successful or how is it so easy to follow Jesus at a young age?" Each time, my response would always be along the lines of, "It is a daily process". I am sure that most of them became aggravated at that broad response, but it is the truth. There is no step by step manual that I can write up to achievement. Life's experiences are our best teachers. Success is a grind. Following Christ at any age is a journey. Everything we put our hands to has necessary steps that you must identify and dedicate to. Anything in life is worth growing through the appropriate changes and stages of development if you want to win.

✓ Waiting While HE Works

"Though one may be overpowered, two can defend themselves. A cord of three strands is not quickly broken"

–Ecclesiastes 4:12 (NIV)

What does waiting look like? How do you wait while God works? How is it that you put yourself in the position to be found by someone if you do not know who is even looking for you?

These were all the questions that pondered in my mind before I met one of the greatest blessings of my young adult life. While healing from one of the worst relationships that I had gone through, I found myself learning to love Shanae again. My heart was flooded with frustration and disappointment. God set me up to discover who I was in Him before He could place anyone in my life. Falling in love with yourself is difficult when there is no sign of its presence in your heart because of what has immorally been done to you in the past. At one point of my life, I had lost my passion to love because I felt as if I kept repeating the same offense of yielding my heart to and trusting the wrong people while continuously getting let down over and over. There came an appropriate time where my heart could not take it anymore, so I decided to take my life back.

During this phase, I struggled with serious issues of developing one of the essential attributes of the fruit of the spirit which was patience. God allowed an amazing and rare gem to cross my path. He has helped with the evolution of who I have become today as the best version of myself. When we met, I was broken, scared, and an emotional wreck. Literally, I was at a desperate moment of needing someone to come into my life as a reliable and focused partner. This man was that and more. At the time of our meeting, we both were living in two separate worlds. He was in ministry and traveling all over the country preaching the Gospel of Jesus Christ, and I was finishing up my bachelor's degree and starting my career as a basketball coach. I know that it was meant for our paths to coincide during a church service on a Sunday morning, and I am so thankful that they did because, since that very day, I have tapped into destiny.

Initially, because of the repeated offenses of looking for love in all the wrong places, and having the expectation of people to fill a void that only God could, I believed he came into my life for that reason. And boy was I wrong. I can remember being so aggressive, impatient, and anxious in our conversations because I thought that is what he wanted and what I needed; but it was so much bigger than that. God allowed this man to come into my life to help me mature the right way through the process of becoming whole. It had nothing to do with him being my Knight in shining armor or being the one to sweep me off my feet. Thankfully, he was sensitive to the voice of God and did not allow my childish ways of thinking that every guy that comes into your life wants to date you, push him away. There were so many times that I almost ruined our friendship by operating in my past way of thinking.

Therefore, it is so important for us as victims of rejection and emotional neglect to advance to a place of wholeness before we try and date someone. You will never properly love the right way, or even know how to be loved the way God designed for a man to love a woman until you do so. This is a part of embracing the process. This season of my life was the most difficult and uncomfortable because I was always accustomed to having things my way and getting them in the time frame that I thought that I deserved. This guy was not like that. He was so controlled and focused. During one of the first conversations we had, I can remember him telling me that he wanted to build himself up through this process and to pace ourselves because he had rushed enough things in his life before and none of it had ever panned out the way that he desired for it to; and this time, if it was going to become something more than friendship, then he was going to take the necessary steps to get there. It was all about embracing the journey.

Honestly, I would become so frustrated, annoyed, and aggravated by what seemed to be a delayed journey between the two of us. I was blinded by my own selfish wants and could not see what God was trying to do and what I had close to me. I finally had the guy that I had always prayed for, just not in the form that I thought it would come through. He was someone who respected me as a woman, and not a trophy or sex object. He grew to love and appreciate my heart and it had nothing to do with what I could give to him physically. I had someone who challenged me in every area of my life and who was accountable in all aspects thereof. He saw my flaws but covered my future. I did not realize at the time that was real love. I had a person who pushed me to become better daily. He was so strategic about everything he did. I honestly fell in love with him the day that I laid eyes on him. I knew that there was something different about him. His walk, his stance, his posture, his approach was authentic. I had for the first time ever in my life, someone to check my character, integrity, and my motives. He made me better. And that is why I had to embrace the process of developing patience.

God thought enough of me during my state of brokenness to send someone who I could develop through the healing process with because he too had baggage as I did. We both needed each other but had to put behind us our past issues to appreciate and value one another to the maximum capacity of who we were evolving to be. One of my favorite authors, Dr. Myles Munroe, said when you make a commitment to something, and people are involved, never commit to the person because they change every day, but your commitment must be to the relationship because it never changes, and that is what we learned and flourished at while doing. It was our method of survival, and it saved our relationship. He and I committed to the journey of helping each other embrace the process.

As past victims of hurt, depression, neglect, and emotional abuse, we should run to the foot of the cross. That is where our healing lies. God can mend any form of brokenness. It is when we go to people and yield our expectations to them that we become powerless and forfeit the rights of wholeness. One thing I admired about my guy is that he always pointed me to Jesus. Naturally, as a woman, I am emotional and when I fell in love, it became systematic and almost second nature to put great expectations on the man not to fail. He would tell me all the time "Shanae I am the most flawed person that I know" and he was right, but even through his flaws, he was perfect for me. God has designed for each of us to win with the right person; trust the process.

Before I accumulated the wisdom to understand why my guy and I had to evolve the way we did, I was so frustrated with not receiving what I thought I needed in the time frame that I desired to have it. God had to show me, that emotionally, I could not handle all that came with being in a healthy relationship because I was still wounded. When we rush in and out of relationships while not becoming properly healed, we ruin anything that may have a slight sign of life because we are dead internally. I am so thankful that I had a man of God who understood my process and did not hold it against me. When seeking to be found by someone, we must trust the strategy of God sending them at the proper time. Anything that is premature and underdeveloped will not provide you with what you need to gravitate towards your purpose.

My friend would not let me slide through any cracks whenever I became emotionally overwhelmed with maneuvering through this stage of learning, loving, respecting, trusting, and more. He would always say, "Getting to know a person takes time; when riding in a car, when you are going slowly, you are able to see much more than when you are driving fast; let's go slow Shanae". Looking back now, I realized that I did not understand it all then because it was so uncomfortable and it challenged my motives and desires which made me mature in more ways than one, but it was probably the best thing to ever happen to me. Having to develop the right way with him also helped in my career field. It was much bigger than just us, but it was about my future as a professional, woman in ministry, mentor, and friend.

We position ourselves to matriculate the right way in relationships by healing properly. Jumping in and out of situations and tying ourselves down to people does not help with this process. That only prolongs the necessary healing of emotional wounds and pushes us further back than where we were initially. You must be mature enough to realize that your life depends on this necessary concept of defining purpose and embracing the journey. Do not harbor the feeling of not wanting to be alone in your heart; that will not allow you to move forward.

Often, the most aggravating part of this journey of learning to wait is most difficult because we put expectations on people that they do not house the capacity to fulfill. In our minds, we formulate how we want things to go instead of learning to trust the plans and strategy of God; we put our own agenda in place and forfeit His, which ends up putting us in a position to fail every time. When you expect people to fill a void that was never meant to be filled by them, then inevitably you have no other choice but to come out without your heart's desire which is to be in a successful and meaningful relationship. Building relationships take time and it's hard work. These foundations are not supposed to be built or founded on premature feelings or false emotions. Many of us are finding ourselves jumping in and out of situations because of our failed attempt to grow through the process of waiting on God to move.

I have learned that I am at my best when I am in the will of God. His plans outweigh mine a million to none. I believed that when I gravitated towards making the conscious decision to live in the moment and stop forcing things in any area of my life. It was then that I could see clearer and began to understand the methods of God placing certain people in my life and taking those who were not needed away. Above anything, I grew to a place in my walk with God to understand that everything He presented to me, ended with making a choice. Just like we choose to get up and start our day, trusting that our vehicles are going to get us to our job, or that our alarm is going to wake us up when it is time to get ready for work, then the same goes for trusting the strategy of God. After something has been tried and tested, then it has proven itself to be worth being believed. I knew that God was a reliable source because of the many times He had come through for me in areas of my life where I had no one to turn to besides Him. Every time I needed Him, He consistently showed up with exactly what I needed.

It was not through turning to my friend or calling on him whenever I needed something, but my foundation of dependency and reliance rested in God. Therefore, I knew that my expectations would always be met. This is the mindset we all should take on, realizing that our worth should never be tied to the hands of people. When we give individuals the capacity to hold our value in their hands, we have just begun a battle that will always lend us a loss. God is our creator. Therefore, He defines our worth, not people or their thoughts of us. That concept ties in with, waiting while He works. You must grow to a place in your life, where you wait on God to move you when He has decided that you are ready. Do not rush what is supposed to last a lifetime. Trust and know that God makes no mistakes, and when the time is right, He will deliver.

✢ *My prayer in the process of Waiting while HE works*

Dear God, I thank you for teaching us how to rely and depend on you even when we do not always understand your methods or your ways. I believe that you make no mistakes, and at the proper time when we are ready to receive our mate, you will allow destiny to meet us in the middle. I thank you for showing us your way and allowing us to abandon our own selfish nature and desires while picking up your ways and developing your thoughts on our own. Thank you, God, for allowing us to rest in peace and patience during this tough process. We believe that you heard our prayers and have honored our petitions by sending us someone to love us even through our most flawed state. I thank you for grooming us during this process and that at the appropriate time, we will reap the harvest because we chose to stand in patience while waiting on you to work. Amen

✓ Building Your FAITH

"For you know that when your faith is tested, your endurance has a chance to grow"

-James 1:3 (NLT)

Faith was one of the most trying areas that I resisted during my walk with God. If things were not going as I wanted or thought they should have been, I was so easily controlled and detoured by my emotions. Being this way caused me to be like an emotional rollercoaster tossed whichever way the curve decided to turn. This was unhealthy and detoxing to my spirit and the nature of who I was as a person naturally. Many of us are this way. Instead of choosing to stand in faith regardless of how things are in our lives, we most often worry ourselves about situations that we have no control over.

As a result of this lack of trust in my belief system that often was based on what was going on or the severity of it, God took me through several tests to grow me to a place of total commitment in standing in faith. One thing I have learned about our belief system is that we have one or two choices. Either we are going to choose to believe God, or we will live in doubt. There is no in between. Often, people say, "Faith and worry cannot dwell in the same place". That is one of the truest statements that I have ever heard. Where I failed was by going back and forth, just depending on how emotionally stable I was at the moment. I would trust and believe God one day, but then the next day, I would allow my emotions to take over or feed me negative thoughts that pushed my faith out the door.

There comes a stable place in your thought process where you choose to starve your fears and feed your faith. No matter what the situation may be or how the odds may be stacked against you, it is either you trust God, or you do not. Think about being in a relationship with someone and you have gained their trust. Although verbally, they say that they trust you, but their actions speak differently, how would that make you feel? I am assuming aggravated or frustrated. God is that way also. We cannot waiver from day to day based on our emotions or when we will decide to trust Him. It is either you do or you do not. We must make up in our minds that we are going to stand either in faith or doubt.

As believers, we cannot stray when circumstances arise in our lives. Adversity is not there to make you doubt who God is, that is the perfect time to rest and dwell on His promises and what His word says. Without tests or trials, then how do we expect to have a testimony of being an overcomer? It is not possible.

The way to build our faith is by existing in God's word. Faith is not conditional or based on how things appear. I said previously in the chapter above, that if you can see the outcome or results, then you do not need faith. It is not based on what we see, but it is dependent on what we know. And we know that all things work together for the good of them who love God and who are called according to His purpose as the book of Romans assures us.

Situations should not dictate our belief system. We must remain anchored and not forget the teachings of His word.

Abiding in faith is a constant process. The only way our faith can remain in a place of pure trust is by infusing those doubts and pressing toward the mark of the high calling which is in Christ Jesus as Paul told us to do in Philippians. Often in our lives, we are like the waves in the sea, constantly being overtaken by the winds of life instead of choosing to be like the rocks in the ocean which are anchored and settled in the sand. His word must continue to be at the forefront of our minds because if not, then it will be impossible to build your faith. Hardships and test come to increase your level of belief in who God is. How will we ever know Him to bring us out of situations that naturally we could not come out of on our own if we do not go through them? That is where building our faith comes in.

When constructing your faith, you have to get to a significant place in your life where you willingly surrender all life's circumstances to God. It's like passing the baton to the runner in front of you because you have run your course of the race. When we yield our issues to Him, then He can do what we do not have the capacity to do on our own. Many of us struggle in this area because of the desire or need to be in complete control. Life has taught me that when following God and remaining in faith, your will is not necessary and will not get you to the destination. The only way that we can live a life pleasing to Him, is by abandoning our will and picking up His. A complete makeover in the mindset is important if you desire to maneuver in this realm of true faith. It does not waiver because of the overwhelming issues that life delivers. This way of thinking disengages from its own understanding but in all its ways, acknowledges God because He is the director of the paths of life.

Leaning on your own will and understanding is a form of self-suicide. Our ways are not like His ways, and His thoughts are higher than our thoughts; therefore, it is impossible to figure out the strategy of God or why He chooses to do the things that He does. When you have faith, there is no need for trying to understand or grasp His plans, just stand and trust Him while allowing Him to do the hard part. Our portion is simple, but we make it complex when taking on a battle that we were never created to handle. His word lets us know that all we must do is stand and allow Him to fight.

One incident occurred in my life during college that grew my faith so strong that I am not sure of what I would have done had I not chosen to abide in faith. God allowed this situation to happen to stretch my belief in His authority in my life. It was two months before my college graduation when my professor, the Dean of the Social Work department sent me an email saying that I was missing a Science course that I needed for graduation and that I would not be able to walk on May 9th. She explained, I would have to wait in the summer to take the course that was missing and could participate in the graduation ceremony in December. The fact that I attended the school for three years and they had just discovered this two months before my graduation was one thing. Second, I was getting ready to take another coaching job in Arkansas at my rival school and I needed my degree to enroll in the Master's program to gain my teaching license.

At that point, I became so overwhelmed. My professor was very helpful and searched all the courses and reached out to some other science teachers to see if I could get an immediate enrollment in the course, but each teacher said that it was too late. Naturally, I wanted to be upset with her, but I could not be. I cried for about a week straight because I felt that my whole life was about to shatter. I remember calling my friend crying one night giving him the details, and he said: "Shanae call me back when you finish crying". At that moment, I was confused and frustrated. I had a hard time understanding why he was being so hard when he knew the severity of the situation and what was at stake. I ended up getting myself together and he told me that tears were not going to change the situation and that I needed to pray and trust God. So, that is what I did.

A month rolled by and still, nothing happened. One day I decided to email the Dean of the Bachelor of Arts department at our University. I explained to him all that had happened and how I just found out that I needed this course. I rendered the details that I had been attending the school for three years seeing an academic advisor each semester. I recalled that their job was to make sure that I had everything I needed to be on course for graduation. I went on to tell him about the job that I was getting ready to take and how I needed my degree to enroll in the graduate program and that was the only way that I would be able to begin this new career. I did not hear back from him for two days, and while I awaited a response I prayed and rested in faith and asked God to move on my behalf.

Two weeks until graduation rolled by. It was a Tuesday morning when the Dean emailed me back and said that he forwarded my request to the President of the university and that they would meet with me the following Thursday to discuss the issue. My heart was pounding with excitement, although I was not sure of what was going to take place, the fact that he responded and said that we would meet was enough for me after not having any answers for almost two months. My desire was not to get any of my professors in any trouble, I just needed something to be done so that I could graduate and move on with my career. The wait began to wear me out emotionally.

Thursday morning came and I was anxious. Before the meeting, I called my mom because I knew that she would pray with me before I went in. She prayed and asked God for favor and that when I left everything would be peaceful and worked out so that I could graduate. After she and I hung up the phone, I felt victory before I entered the Dean's office. Once his secretary called me and my professor back to his office I was no longer nervous. I believed with all my heart that if God allowed it to come this far that the Dean of the entire department scheduled a meeting with me to see what he could do so that I could graduate, then all would be well. Standing a week before graduation, not having been able to order my cap and gown yet because of the opposition sitting in front of me, I chose to stand in faith.

The three of us sat down and pulled up my transcript of all the classes that I had taken at the university and the previous one that I had transferred from. While the head Dean of the department and my professor talked things over and surveyed my transcript, I sat there praying in my heart asking God to grant my request. The day we met was the last day for graduates to enroll in the exit program to be released from the university and sign the promissory note saying that they would follow up with their student loans after graduation. The last session had to meet at 12:30, and I was currently in the meeting working out my situation at 11:30. While they worked on a solution, I just kept praying that something would come together and that I would be able to get across campus to make it to that meeting and sign my paperwork.

As they began to wrap up their conversation, my professor smiled and said: "I think we may have found a way to fix it." My heart leaped for joy. They were able to pull two courses that I had taken at my previous college to stand in the gap for the course that I needed in order to graduate from my current university. When I say, God came through for me when nothing else seemed as if it was going to work. I had no idea that I had taken that science class. When they pulled the transcript up and read the description of what we did and the necessary components, it identically matched the class that I needed. The course was just named something else. I ran out of the office after I hugged both the Dean of the department and my professor and screamed thank you Jesus to the parking lot as I ran across the street to make it to the session. We ended the meeting at 12:24.

I was able to purchase my cap and gown and register for graduation that same day. I stood in faith and the following Friday walked across the stage as my mom's first college graduate. Although I did not end up taking the job back in Arkansas, I did enroll in the graduate program to begin my Masters. God strategically set me up, even though the plans that I had thought I was getting ready to make did not pan out, there was yet purpose in it all. God pushed me to a place where no one could get the credit in that situation but Him. He used someone who did not know me or my situation but allowed them to open the door for me to have a testimony. Those are the kind of things that God will do for us once we remove ourselves from the situation and allow him to be who He says He is.

God had to push me to a place where I had only one option and that was to trust Him. There was nothing or no one to turn to besides Him and that is where He wants us to be as believers in the body of Christ. Those moments position us to grow and increase our level of faith and expectancy in Him. Even after that trial happened, there followed many more that were even greater in the magnitude of difficulty. None of them came to make me doubt God or to throw in the towel and give up, but they were strategically set in place to mature me in the walk of faith. When we rest in peace while knowing that come what may, if God cannot do it, then it cannot be done, then that is a pure sign of true belief. Our confidence should always rest in God; not in people or our ability to get things done, because without Him, we are nothing. It is in Him that we live, move, and have our being. Our whole world should center on that piece. I finally arrived at a place of total commitment and trust in my belief system. My dependence on God began to grow and the more I was tried in the fire, the stronger I grew in faith.

✢ *My prayer as you learn to grow through the process*

Dear God I thank you for these believers who stand in faith and choose to trust you with the plans of their lives. We believe that you will give us the strength to embody where we are headed and that as we move along this tedious journey that you will properly give us the grace to endure the many tests that shall arise. I thank you because we will not be moved by our situations or shaken because of the currents of life, but we will stick it out and go through the necessary stages in order to get us to the place you have designed for us to be. We believe these things in your name, Amen.

❖ Chapter 4:

The Middle

"Success is to be measured not so much by the position that one has reached in life as by the obstacles which he has overcome while trying to succeed"

-Booker T. Washington

The middle of circumstances is seemingly where the pressure of outlasting what has you on the downside, begins to increase to a greater extent in intensity. In this position, we have options. We can turn and go back, or continue to press beyond where we currently are. This ramification does not dictate where we are headed, and usually has nothing to do with who we are. In between your breakthrough and harvest are your birthing pains. At this point, comes the realization that we have endured too much to turn back. Keep moving.

✓ *TRAILBLAZING towards Victory*

"I have told you these things so that in me you may have peace. In this world, you will have trouble. But take heart! I have overcome the world"

–John16:33 (NKJV)

In the moment of feeling as if you are not advancing towards your desired goal, is the official opportunity to project oneself to the destination. We should understand that with the irritating place in which we have become resentful towards, its intent is to strengthen us for the journey ahead. Our eyes ought to remain fixed on what lies in front of us. Every bit of who we are blossoming into should signify and replicate our preparation. Imperfect seasons should not destroy our ambition. We serve a perfect God who has the power to give us authority over our situations.

Upon takeoff, each passenger will experience a little discomfort as the airplane excels from altitude to altitude. In that instant, individuals who have experienced flying do not become frantic because they have built resistance to the turbulence. First-time flight attendants, however, may initially panic or become frightened but cannot abort the ride because they are secured for the journey. Often, God elevates us, but He makes sure that we are sustained so that we will not abandon where we are headed as a result of the adversity that is attached to the ride. Alongside each proportion of growth in life, we can expect some displeasure. It is important that we do not interrupt our arrival out of unfamiliarity or because of experiencing a little affliction. Advancement creates being in undesirable situations, but they only last for a temporary season.

The worst part about losing basketball games for me as a young rookie head coach was having to bypass the fans while heading to the locker room. Those bystanders, witnessed us fall short in our competition, and it became difficult for me as the coach to hold myself together from frustration with our efforts. Although I was irritated with the way we may have performed or failed to do so, that could not diminish my love, passion, and drive to still say positive things about my girls or our program when fans approached me after a loss. It was easier for them to point out our mistakes, but as a coach who took pride in everything that embodied my team, I would always say, "We know what we have to work on". That is all a part of having their back and understanding that even losses have a way of redirecting our focus. Defeat is based on a mindset.

Losses do not define who you are, and they definitely should not force you to stop progressing forward. This fight has many dynamics attached to it that demands your presence physically, mentally, and emotionally. Again, do not give up out of fear of failing; there is no failure in God. Therefore, failure is not an option on this journey. We learn from our testimonies.

During my second year of coaching at Lee Academy, my junior high team was very young and inexperienced. We had a little success and found ourselves entering the district tournament seeded number four. Because of that, we were to face the number five team, who we had previously beaten twice during the regular season meetings. Although that was our case, from previous experience as a player, I did not have my mind fixed on the fact that we had beaten them twice. I knew that anything was possible with the game of basketball and just about anything could happen on any given night. What it boils down to is who has prepared the most and desires to advance more than the other opponent. I made sure that I explained this concept to my girls before the game and during our preparation for the team before the tournament. Even their parents talked with much confidence because it seemed as if we had the upper hand. I remained humble because I remember during my collegiate year at Delta State, we as the number nine team that was ranked in the nation of the Division II Women's Basketball association fell short to a team that we had previously beaten by forty plus points. Anything can happen.

That night, we fell short to the team that we had previously beaten badly. That was a humbling experience for us. I believe that my girls needed to feel that so that it could bring awareness to what I kept trying to reiterate to them before we faced this opponent for the third time. My head coach in college always would say, it is so difficult to beat a team three times. And he was right. It was. After falling short to that relentless and tenacious team, I knew that my girls would never want to have that feeling again. It made us focus more on the upcoming season. That offseason was the most productive that we had since I was at the school. No one gave an excuse for wanting to get out of the workouts. That loss ignited something deep down in us and brought us closer together. Adversity builds character.

The following year, the tables had turned. We found ourselves seeded fifth after some tough losses and some that we should have ended with a win. But they always say everything happens for a reason, and as I have matured in this profession, I believe that also. Being the fifth seed, we had to face the fourth-place team in the district tournament. Ironically, that team was the same exact opponent that had beaten us in last year's district tournament. And again, we were on the opposite side of the playing field. They now just as we had the upper hand on them, had beaten us twice during the regular season matchups. Neither game was close. They single-handedly beat us. This team had confidence going into the tournament, but deep down I believed that the situation was in our favor because of what we had experienced the previous year in losing to them which ended our season early.

The pregame speech that I had given to the girls was simple. First, I asked if they remembered the feeling we had after that loss last year. Each one expressed with great emotion that they could never forget what it felt like. My next question was if they believed the opposing team had much respect for us taking into consideration the last three times we had faced them we came out on the downside. The last thing I told my girls, as I looked all nineteen of them in the eye individually and called them by name, was "I believe in you". That night, we played with a fire that I had never seen. They had an incredible athlete on the opposing team that was ranked as the leading scorer in our conference. She was something to watch. The player averaged 15 points per game. Against us that night she only had four. Our team played in harmony and with soul. My heart was so proud of their efforts to compete. We finished the game with a twelve-point lead against an opponent that had every reason to believe that they would defeat us. We chose to continue to move toward the terminal.

That game had several life lessons attached to it. I believe that at that moment, my girls learned to weather the storm and persevere through adversity. Times are going to be rough. Things are not always what they appear to be. Most importantly, we learned that it is possible to defeat a giant that you may have failed to once or even twice in your life. Each time we are faced with opposition, we must know that it births a new opportunity to gain a different result. But we first must have a renewed and changed mindset. The race is not given to the swift or the battle to the strong, but to those who endure to the end. Keep moving. Keep fighting. Victory is on the other side of your battle. Life does not come to a standstill because of our failures. No one will feel sorry for you at the hand of defeat. Those moments grow us and mature our ability to excel beyond where we have come up short. It is imperative that we overtake the situation by its horns and ride it out.

This thing that we call life will afford us some of the most intentional unexpected experiences and if we embrace all that comes with it, I believe that it will grant us the access to rise above our ashes. Be steadfast and remain in good hope knowing that the worst is behind and the best is straight ahead. You must continue to pursue purpose.

✝ *My prayer for the navigation towards victory.*

Today, I declare that you step out in faith knowing fully well that there is no battle too hard for God. It is my prayer that each of you maneuver beyond any setback, disappointment, or heartache that has come to blind you from pursuing your NEXT. I pray that you begin to desire the more of God and that through this establishment of relationship; He opens doors that no one can shut. I believe that God can do anything, and through this prayer by your faith, no matter the circumstance that arises in your life, I decree that you are more than a conqueror through Christ Jesus who gives you strength. Amen.

✓ Living through the Defeated MOMENT

"Being defeated is often a temporary condition. Giving up is what makes it permanent"

-unknown

Once upon a time, I was afraid of living on purpose with purpose. That simply means, thriving in the moment and whatever comes with the given opportunity, take it for exactly what it is. Too many times we forget that principle. As believers, we should manifest where we are and prepare for where we are headed. That constitutes a reconciled mindset that is set on positive and joyful manners of life. No matter the difficulty that may be extended to us from our situations, there is an extensive need to press beyond.

Such concepts as lingering in the past will not spare us benefits to the set place that has strategically been assigned to our lives. There must come a premeditated choice where we decided to own the rights that have been granted to us by God. Liberty in our mind and wholeness from the neglect is what we have access to. Joy in moments that seemingly appear as if there lies no hope. Forgiveness from our mistakes. These are attributes of the birthright. It is His desire and goodwill that we prosper in this way. Believe it. Receive it. Go after it!

Do you believe in miracles? At this point of my frustrating, at times discouraging life, full of detours, roadblocks, and disappointments, I found myself prospering in my purpose. I told you earlier that I did not receive the job in Arkansas after I graduated from college. That season of my life was one of the greatest tests of adversity and hardship that I had ever experienced.

One day I received a call from the head girls' basketball coach in Hamburg which was my rival school. He told me that he was preparing to retire and needed someone to replace him. Coach Martin went on to explain that this upcoming group was special and that he wanted the right person to take over the program. While listening to him talk, all I could think of is why would he call me? He and I had never had a conversation before. After every game when we played against his team in high school, the most he would say to me in passing as we shook hands was, "*good game*

Govan". I had no clue how he got my number or why after five years since I had graduated from high school he would call me after all the great players he had coached personally.

He ended the conversation by asking if I would be willing to take over his position and get the program in the right direction. We set up a meeting between me, him, and the Superintendent of the school for that following Thursday. After he and I hung the phone up, I was so confused. I could not figure out what just happened or why. Immediately, I began to pray and ask God for direction. The next week, I found myself packing and telling my current team that I had committed to taking a job back in Arkansas and that I was moving that week. I felt like I heard God say *"yes"*.

I moved back home and left my current job in Mississippi to come and accept a job that I had never officially got. I was confused, hurt, lost, and overwhelmed. There was one huge component that stood in my way, and that was passing the Praxis II exam to receive my teaching licensure. In the state of Arkansas, the only way you can coach at a public school is by having a teaching license. There was a Master's of Art in teaching program that I had to enroll in to get this degree. I was immediately accepted and began my courses. In addition to being in the program, non-traditional teachers like myself had to pass three tests to stay in the program and to remain hired by the school of choice.

The superintendent liked me so much after our first meeting and told me that he would give me the entire summer to pass all the tests, and said that I could begin practicing with the girls in the meantime because he had faith that the job belonged to me. I passed all the required tests besides the content and knowledge which was the actual licensure test. The other two were easy. I took it twice and failed both times. Feeling defeated I became worried and frantic out of fear of what lied ahead. A month rolled by and I still had not passed the test.

At this point, I became extremely stressed because I knew if I had not passed by the time of the summer ending, then I could not begin the school year as the head girls' basketball coach. How embarrassing is what I thought. I mean everyone knew about me "verbally" committing to this job, but what if I failed and could not take it was all that kept ringing in my head. I felt dumb and inadequate. Everyone in my hometown was in disbelief and some even were upset when they found out that I had committed to this job. Hamburg and Crossett were big rivals that naturally hated each other. But, my point was that I did not apply for this position. It came and found me.

Before I moved from Mississippi and had verbally said that I was going to accept this new opportunity, in the back of my heart, I was skeptical. We had accomplished so much during my first year as a head coach while juggling finishing up my bachelor's degree and fighting the dynamics of being young, inexperienced, and black in a racially divided place. My girls grew on me. We made history twice that year and had achieved more than had been in decades. And now, I was faced with a chance to walk away from it all. The headmaster who hired me, expressed in a conversation before I left that if it did not work out that I could always come back. He prayed with me before I made the final decision and said if I ever needed anything to always reach out. That was true love. Although it would put them in a rough spot to find a new coach, he just wanted me to be happy. I thought I was making the right decision at the time.

I can recall some of the reaction of my girls when I told them that I was leaving. Their parents were shocked and sad. Everyone could not believe that I was leaving after the success that I had brought to the school. People whom I did not coach or have their kid in my class reached out and expressed their disbelief when they found out that I was leaving. That brought a great level of awareness of how much I was appreciated. It felt so awesome to receive those calls and text messages from everyone who told me of the impact I had made on their community and school in such short amount of time.

As time grew closer to August, I had one last attempt to pass the test. I studied day and night. I even reached out to my friends who had previously taken the same exam. Each of them explained how stressful and difficult it was for them to pass and how it took them a year or two to prepare and even pass it. Those individuals were also majors in this department, and I was a nontraditional student, looking to pass within two and a half months.

My boss from my former school called me on a Sunday evening and told me that he needed a favor. He expressed that his mom had been in the hospital as she was during the time that I was at Lee. No one had been hired in my place. Because of this, he needed me to take the girls to a basketball camp that upcoming Monday and Tuesday because he did not have anyone else to do so. Of course, I was going to do it. After all he had done for me, how could I not. Here it was a Sunday, that I had to drive to Mississippi for two days and coach my former team in a basketball camp, study for a test that I needed to pass and had to take for the final time on the upcoming Friday, while trying to manage my emotions and deal with the "what ifs" of the situation. After taking the exam on that Friday, I was headed to Florida for a much-needed vacation with my friend Brittany.

I took the girls to the basketball camp and they were so excited. The night before the game, we all texted back and forth in the group chat speaking about our excitement to be back in the groove for one last time. At the tournament, we ended up winning our games and had a blast just like old times. When I got back to Arkansas and took the test that Friday, I prayed and asked God for his will to be done. I told him that I wanted an answer regarding what to do when I came back from the vacation with my best friend. Sitting at the computer while taking the exam I felt like a champion. As I read and answered each question I became more and more confident as I continued toward the end. The questions seemed easier than before when I had previously taken it. Usually, once you take the test, it will tell you right there if you passed or failed. Mine did not this time. I stood in anticipation as I got up from the desk not knowing what to tell the Superintendent.

I called him on my way home, and he answered the phone and said: "Tell me something good Coach G". I told him about the score not posting immediately as it should have done and he reassured me that it would be fine. He said that I should be expecting an email within the next few days and that the computer sometimes does that in different situations. I did not know whether that was a good or bad thing considering the fact that I was headed on vacation and unaware of what my next move was going to be.

I made it back to my hometown and Brittany was waiting for me at my mom's house. I was already packed and mentally over with everything. On the way to Florida, I was so weighted with pressures of what was about to take place. Once we made it after those seven hours, I was so physically, mentally, and emotionally drained that I did not want to do anything besides rest my mind. Thankfully, my friend understood what I was dealing with and decided that she would use that day as a rest day also. I promised her that I would not worry during the trip and ruin our fun because of what was going on. I did not want to be selfish and make the whole vacation revolve around my situation. I decided to leave it all to God. There was nothing else left for me to do besides trust Him, and so I did.

The following day, we went to the beach. I laid out and processed the entire situation. While in the midst of prayer, I heard the voice of God so clear and precise whisper, "I'm not finished". I immediately jumped up and became nervous. I knew what I heard but was not sure why I heard it or what it meant. Impatiently, I ran over to where Brittany was laying down on the sand soaking her feet on the bank and told her what had just happened. She smiled and replied so peacefully, "well go back to Mississippi Shanae". I can remember how nonchalantly she stated it as if she had already known that this move was going to happen and the outcome of it. I told her that it was not that simple and how do I know that is what God meant or if I could even get my job back. She said, God has it all worked out and what will be, will be.

I pondered on what to do next for the rest of the day. I concluded that Brittany was right. I made a decision. Stepping out in faith, when I made it back to the hotel that night I made the most challenging phone call of my adult life. There I was not knowing if I passed the Praxis II or not, but I was in the process of calling my old boss to ask him if I could come back home and take my job back. At that moment, I was not consumed with the opinions of others or the rumors that would spread about what happened. All I knew was that I heard God and I had to be obedient to His voice.

My headmaster answered his phone so eagerly and with such excitement in his voice as if he knew why I was calling. I could see the grin on his face through the phone. Immediately following his *"hello"* I asked could I have my job back if he had not filled the position yet. He laughed and said he knew deep down that I would be back and he could not find anyone to replace me! I was so overjoyed and elated. I made one phone call to the family that opened the door for me to have the job in the first place that I had met three years prior to moving to Clarksdale; the Chrestmans'. As I began to tell Big J about returning, the entire household erupted in cheers. I guess once I hung up, they called everyone in town and got the word out because my phone began to ring off the hook. My cell blew up with text messages asking if it was true. Parents stated that it was the best news they had received all summer. I was so happy. God had my back during the entire process.

I waited until I returned from Florida to tell the girls at Hamburg. We had grown so close in such a small amount of time. Some of the girls began to attend my hometown church with me on Wednesdays for Bible Study and even on Sunday mornings. I was connected to them very rapidly but had an assignment to be fulfilled in Mississippi. That's basically how I explained it to them when we had our final team meeting upon my arrival. The following Sunday we all decided to say our goodbyes at my church as a team farewell fellowship. They were so sweet and thoughtful to have organized a presentation in honor of me during the church service. I was so shocked but thankful. Those three months with them were life-changing. Although our chapter had ended sooner than expected, I kept in touch with them all after I transitioned back to Mississippi. For some of them, I became an advocate in their life. I looked at it as a temporary season that God allowed me to go to Hamburg for a short time, and it had nothing to do with basketball. It was laced with opening the door to connect me with some of those girls who needed someone who would believe in them and help push them to a place of wholeness.

When I moved back, no one asked questions about what happened. They were all just so glad that I returned and we could start as if we had never departed. A family that I had never met even offered to allow me to move into one of their rent houses, "rent free". They said they had watched the impact that I had on the student body before I left and just wanted to be a blessing to my ministry. I did not feel appreciated before I left. Once I made the transition to come back it was as if it went to an exceeding level above my expectations. Everyone was so excited that I was back and it showed. Above all, I was respected and loved which is all you can ask for especially being associated with the dynamics that I had been in for about two years.

God even allowed me to become a youth minister when I went back to Clarksdale. Here it was I began leading bible study every Tuesday night to middle school students of about sixty to seventy per night. I knew that I had begun living on purpose. Had I stayed in Arkansas, I would not have had the opportunity to proceed in this new way created by God. It was greater than just the game. Morgan Freeman had recently written a documentary on how racism and segregated things were still in Mississippi; and here it was I was the first African American coach and teacher at this private school in his hometown while also leading bible study to the wealthy, educated, and white students. That's *Purpose*. Thankfully, I did not get offset by the opposition placed in front of me with the test situation. Taking that job was not a part of the destination; it was just a passing terminal.

Those hardships and disappointments helped develop this tough shell surrounding my emotions that had a huge part in teachable moments that I had to go through to arrive at this safe place. Most of the time, difficult seasons are attached to advancement; but we must first be willing to withstand the test. It is because of these life lessons that we grow to appreciate God for always being a life jacket in the storm. No matter how hard the wind may blow, God is still there with His long arm and strong hand in anticipation to pull us through and beyond the adversity.

There will come times where we become blinded by our opposition, and that is the perfect time to surrender it to Him, and trust that where He guides, He will surely provide a way of escape.

✣ *My prayers to embark and live through your defeated moment.*

God, you said in your word that you will never put more on us than we can bear and that all things work together for the good of them who love you and who are called according to your purpose. I thank you because I know that your word is activated in each believer's life and that you will allow your sons and daughters to rest in knowing that you will never leave them in despaired moments. God give them the grace to continue to pursue those dead miracles and trust you while in pursuit of the manifested glory that will be revealed through your word. I thank you for each person reading this and by faith, they will LIVE through their defeated moments. In your name we pray, Amen.

✓ Advancing BEYOND the Comfortable Place

"We are hard-pressed on every side but not crushed; perplexed, but not in despair. Persecuted but not abandoned; struck down but not destroyed"

–II Corinthians 4:8-9 (NKJV)

At the appropriate time of our landing, it is important for us not to confuse what was only meant to be for a set "season" in our lives, with what is congruent to our *"destiny"*. Seasons are conditional. This means, as a result of what transpired, there was a designated cause for me to have to go through all that I did so that I could get to my destination. My forever. Purpose is congruent to specific seasons and situations. It is a premature destiny that has not been fulfilled yet. Many times, we magnify the fact that something has "potential" and become stagnated at this temporary place, and instead never grow or press further towards the greater place, which is destiny! This thing births out in you what you will need to get to your future, but is not all the time meant to go with you to your destination.

Look at Moses. He birthed another level of purpose into Joshua and instilled effective leadership qualities in him, but was not able to go to the destination because he was not connected to the destiny of the promise land. Had Moses gone, Joshua would not have walked into his future. He could not go because it would have prevented the promise. It is vital that we do not allow our destiny to be prohibited or altered because of the desire to take something only meant for a season into our harvest place. We will not be able to mature or advance to our designed assignment on earth.

Destiny is yours forever. It says that no matter what happens, I am connected to each altitude of purpose and am not seasonal or based on a certain situation. I am the forever. It goes from season to season flourishing within its well-thought-out plan because it is a matured state of being. With people that are tied and joined to your destiny, your durability is congruent with their existence. It says that the two of you are willing and must evolve with one another from destination to destination. You are bonded to this individual because your forever has been written in destiny.

Without Sarah, Abraham would not have been the father of Isaac. He needed her, even in her old age to birth out and fulfill his predestinated assignment. His obedience to the voice of God included Sarah. Abraham could not abandon their home and go to a foreign land without also taking the one who was unified with his destiny. She was carrying his seed of purpose. He could not start a new beginning with anyone else, and be called "the father of many nations". Because his destiny was tied to Sarah, she had to birth out their purpose in the earth.

Sarah doubted the voice of God and went beneath His plans and convinced her husband to sleep with Hagar. Their current circumstance did not change the will of God. What He spoke continued to be in motion, regardless of the plot to undermine and devalue the word that had been released. Nevertheless, Ishmael was conceived and was Abraham's first son, but he was not the PROMISE child. Sarah still had to evolve and grow to understand that she was commanded to fulfill God's promise because she had the keys to Abraham's destiny. There was no way around what God had already spoken into the earth. She was connected to the destination and establishment of Abrahams's destiny.

Everything we have gone through up until this point has all been a significant piece of the Master Plan designed by God. It has only been for your making. He has been your strength like no other reaching to you even through the toughest situations that have occurred at this point. Sarah's situation looked as if there was no way that she could fulfill the promise that God gave to her concerning giving birth to a son.

Purpose births out in us all the necessary components that we will need to gain another level of shielding for our next place. Just like a rocket, before it takes off, there are several parts of the shuttle that will not get to go through the next phase surpassing the ozone layer. If the shuttle does not make the proper drop-off, then it will prohibit its safer and more secure push out towards its destination. This is the mindset we should pursue when chasing after destiny! For each monument of growth constitutes a "Drop Off".

Alleviate the negative, disapproving, or unsure thoughts that may surface in your mind when taking this step. It is important to realize how far we have already come and the steps that have been made to get us to this significant place in our lives. One must know and remember that this journey denotes constant change, growth, and acceptance of all that will arise during this point of destiny. When God breaks us, He does it with grace. He allows certain circumstances to plow up in our lives, not to hurt us but its sole purpose is to help place you in the position to rise from your ashes. Being broken signifies that you are made available to begin the process of being poured into. But before this can take place in your life, it is important that you dismantle everything that is preoccupying unnecessary space within your heart.

Had I not gone through the necessary steps that it took to get me to the position that I rest in now at twenty-five years old as the head girls' basketball coach in my hometown; I would have forfeited all the rights to my destination. Yes, it took all that had transpired in not being able to start the job in Hamburg, being rejected and mishandled by parents at my first school, losing myself in one of the most toxic relationships that I had ever been in, denied by a job because I failed a test and more. All of these things built me for this day. Through it all, I know that God was preparing me for this moment in time. Although I was in the midst of trials and tribulations, His word was still in motion. Those circumstances that were attached to my life did not change what His word and promises said concerning me. It all was a part of the Master Plan.

There came a deep hunger and willingness to press beyond the mountain. Those adversities had to happen. In the valley is where we are developed and molded for our mountaintop. The valley experiences enable individuals to discover their destiny. Anyone can maneuver and excel when life is going well or when everything fits systematically. But it is during the chaos and dysfunctional seasons where all hope is lost and there is nothing to rely on besides the word of God and your faith in knowing that if He cannot do it, then it cannot be done. Often, we tap out before our time. There comes an essential desire to press above the frustration of not understanding why certain things have occurred. We must know that it is all for our making. When we don't grow on our own, life will gift us a crisis.

Again, I found myself traveling on my way back to Mississippi after being home on a weekend with family. It was a Monday morning around seven thirty and I was in the process of telling God to give me a sign of what my next assignment was going to be. I knew that my time was expiring at Lee Academy, and I believed that He was pleased with my efforts in modeling Him for the past three years. While in the process of talking to Him, and asking questions about my next endeavor, I received a phone call that would change my life forever.

I did not recognize the number, but the caller I.D. said Crossett, Arkansas. I immediately thought, it could have been my dad from his work office number, but never in a million years did I believe it would be what it turned out to be. I answered the phone with pose, and the guy on the other end introduced himself as the Superintendent of the Crossett School District. He said, "I know you do not know me, but I have heard a lot of great things about you and was wondering if you would be interested in considering the head girls' basketball job". My heart dropped to my feet, and I smiled and told him that I honestly had no aspirations of moving back home. He said that the job had been open for several months and that they had interviewed several people but everyone in the community kept saying, "Shanae Govan is who you need". My heart dropped again. At the moment when I asked God to give me direction on my next assignment, I got a phone call in seconds with a job offer, and not just any opportunity, but one that was congruent to where I had made a big enough impact as a student-athlete in high school that still had a lasting impression on everyone. I stood in awe.

The conversation ended with us scheduling a meeting for the following Friday in the town that I had called home. The entire week, I wrestled with God. Thoughts began to resurface about what had transpired in Hamburg and how I thought that I heard Him then and I told God that I could not take another hit like I did the last time. Although He came to my rescue I did not believe that if it did not work out this time that I could go back to Clarksdale, this time it had to be the real thing. My heart could not take another blow as such. I survived it, but if I was going to transition out, I wanted it to be in His will; the safest place to be.

That entire week, I prayed and analyzed every possible scenario about returning home. I did not know any of the upcoming kids. Public schools are so different than private schools. My youth ministry was a huge factor because I knew if I took this job, then I could no longer teach bible study to my students because of the code of ethics violations. That was a lot. My favorite group that I had become attached to in my three years at Lee were in their last year of high school, and one player Lexi Mitchell, I knew that she would be devastated because I was literally her anchor. I had no clue of how to tell the girls, my boss, or their parents. I had previously done this to them before and did not know if I could do it again. In the back of my heart, I knew that time was up. My heart left that school six months before this phone call had happened, but being in the process of deciding was difficult. After the emotional battle ended, and I decided that if the interview went well, and if I liked the Superintendent, then I was going to give it a shot. I had nothing to lose. It was time for a new beginning. Seven years had passed since I graduated from Crossett High, and now going into year eight, it signified purpose.

The day of the interview I had to speak at a youth conference in Lacy Arkansas. My topic to the young people was "Committing to the Journey". I told them that there are three things that let you know if you are committed to the journey or not. Those things were our connections, choices, and commitment. We talked about the dynamic of being entangled with the wrong people which affects our choices and commitment to doing what it takes to remain on the right path towards our destination. In the process of ministering to them, I had no time to ponder on the interview. At that moment, my focus was on mentoring a group of millennials who have been tossed to the side and forgotten about. And it was in that instant, that I realized I was living in purpose.

Our youth conference was supposed to last for two sessions, but I had the interview in between both sessions. Crossett was about a thirty-minute drive from Lacey. I figured the interview would last only an hour so I told Elder Giles that I would be back in time for the second session. Little did I know that I would be in a three-hour interview discussing "Life" with my new boss. Immediately when I arrived in my hometown, there came a sense of peace that fell upon my heart. A new beginning. When I entered the administration building, I was greeted with "welcome home" by the office secretary. It was as if everyone had already heard the news and was anticipating my acceptance of the job. I already felt at home and had not sat down with the Superintendent yet. *Purpose.*

I was asked to have a seat because he had stepped out for a moment. While sitting with great anticipation, I said one last prayer, *"Lord if this is you, show me"*. I closed my eyes and envisioned coaching on the sideline in the gym where my legacy as a player remains as the best girls' basketball player to have played at CHS being the only one to have signed a basketball scholarship in the school's history. Several guys had signed scholarships and gone off to play, but never a girl; besides me. And now I was faced with the opportunity to change that. I had the opportunity to help develop the next, "Shanae Govan" to make history. The daydreaming finally wore off when I heard a doorknob twist and behind it, I made eye contact with a huge smile and friendly face. "This is it" were the thoughts that bomb-rushed my mind. "Come on back", he said.

I knew the moment I walked into the conference room, that my decision had been made. I literally was sitting in purpose without having said one word about his expectations or what he was looking for in the person to fill the position. We began the conversation by acknowledging that he and I were both student-athletes of Arkansas Tech University so there was an immediate attraction in our conversation. Although I did not graduate from there as he did, we still talked as if we were alumni of the same school. I expressed to him the impact the university had on my ability to push beyond frustrating moments. It was there that I experienced one of the toughest valleys of my life in athletics and with my first college coach. Those two years developed me for where I was headed.

The Superintendent and I talked for three hours, not all consumed with basketball; but mainly about life. While we talked, I reflected on my life and at that moment realized why I had to grow through the adversity, disappointments, and setbacks. He and I expressed to one another the importance that coaches have on student-athletes. Thankfully, he had a background in coaching basketball and had experience as a referee for several years of the game so he understood more than the average administrator who typically is not as involved in athletics. That made our conversation more engaging. I was so thankful that he extended the opportunity and listened to my heart. I was asked questions about my upbringing and philosophy of life. I began to convey what basketball taught me about life. That game helped develop a fire that has never gone out. I told Mr. Williams that I wanted to come back and pour into our community and that if I took this job it was bigger than just being the girls' basketball coach. This movement was about fulfilling purpose.

As the meeting came to an end, I realized that I had to drive back to Lacey and finish the second session of the youth day. He asked what was prepared for the rest of the evening as we shook hands and began to part ways, and I told him about the engagement that was yet to be fulfilled. He smiled and said that was confirmation that he made the right decision in calling me on that Monday morning. As I drove back to complete the assignment that I left before the interview, I stood in awe of how good God was. He was strategic with placing people around me who believed in my abilities to lead a generation to their next destination through coaching the game that I loved.

Once I made it back to Lacey, the young people were so glad to see me return. I initially forgot what I was going to speak to them about previously before the interview so I just decided to wing it. We ended the assignment by becoming empowered to win. Not just in athletics, but in life. I told them to be obedient to their parents and to listen in school. The choices that we make today shape our world tomorrow. It was expressed that life is going to be tough and the decisions we make today have a significant impact on the destination. Those kids were so focused and keyed in on every word that I was saying. Each one was making eye contact and their body language was positive. I knew that this was the start of a new beginning.

God had kept me away from my hometown for seven years. That number represents completion. Going into this eighth year as the new girls' basketball coach signified a new beginning. It was a fresh start to something that would shape a culture and reinforce change and hope. This moment in time was bigger than me. My life was attached to the lives of students who needed a role model, mother figure, advocate, counselor, and more. This was the birthing of a new journey that had everything to do with peace, prosperity, and positivity; and it was just beginning to make sense. The destination was closer than what I thought.

✝ *My prayer as you look to go beyond the comfortable place in your life*

God, I lift everyone up right now who may be struggling with stepping out on faith and moving towards their greater place in you. I thank you because I know that you will unlock their gifts and allow it to make room for them. It is my prayer that you will show each person where their strength lies and that they will make the decision to trust you as they grow to a deeper level in faith knowing that you can do anything but fail. Help your son and daughter who may be fighting against pursuing after dead dreams out of fear of failing. Allow them to know that there is no failure in you and that you make all things well. Remind them that you will perfect all things concerning us and that you said that we are the Head and not the tail, above and not beneath. It is my prayer that each person grows to the maximum of their potential and break out of this comfortable place. In your name we pray, Amen.

❖ CHAPTER 5:

THE DESTINATION

"I consider that our present sufferings are not worth comparing with the glory that will be revealed in us"

–Romans 8:18 (NIV)

The arrival to the place that everyone so desperately anticipates even before their journey begins. It has all been tangible to where your feet are planted now. At the appropriate time, God always shows up with his strong hand to deliver you from the thing that appeared to have more power than you. Our mindsets must be connected to what His word says about our situation. We must pursue past our pain. It is only for a moment to birth in us what we have been in desperate need of.

Once our feet are settled in unfamiliar territory, the thought that continues to resurface in our minds, is "what's next". This place is foreign. It's unborn and the only way to survive is to be totally led by the hand of God. There must be a commitment to recognize that this new province has a great need of total abandonment of our will. His word is a compass that leads us like the northern star. Before there were maps or GPS' all that individuals traveling on a journey had to rely on were the stars. We have transitioned and now have the word of God to be our navigation on the road to our destiny.

The desertion that we have encountered to get to this place has been nothing but a sign of being God's selection. Just as He decided to choose Joseph to be denied by his very own brothers and sold into slavery, He also chose you to go through challenges in order to reach the safe place called "Destiny". Had it not been for Joseph being sold into captivity, and thrown into the pit, he would not have made it to the palace. Our isolated and devastating moments have created in us what we will need to survive at the port of call. It took the anguish and days where you felt that things could only get worse to get you to this place. Our valley moments position our hearts to appreciate when we have outlasted the things that were set out to destroy us.

God strategically had to allow certain circumstances to arise in our lives to dismantle the unnecessary baggage that we have carried. Had we not abandoned those things, we would have prohibited ourselves from advancing to the PROMISE land. When God breaks us, He does it gracefully. Trials come to help us grow to another level in our faith and mature our being. We must remain pure in heart and trust the plans of God because even when we make our arrival to this most prepared place, if our minds are not in sync with moving with the desires of God, then we will not succeed.

✓ *Dividing the ASSETS from liabilities*

"Listen to advice and accept discipline, and at the end, you will be counted among the wise"

–Proverbs 19:20 (NIV)

At last, we have come to a resting place in our lives to finally embrace where we are, to secure where we are headed. Many times in this race, it is so easy to get thrown off course; often, there comes the opportunity to become so frustrated with the race itself instead of choosing to rest in believing that we are safe in His arms. At this point, have you accomplished the desires of your heart? What impact have you left on individuals? Are there any unanswered questions that you are harboring in your mind? As believers on this journey, we should understand that the safest place to abide is in the will of God. All the things we have gone through to get to this portion of the destination have been orchestrated by Him. For us to continue in this way, we must press beyond and know that we are secure.

It is vital that once we arrive at this anticipated destination that we do not allow the daily affairs of life to distract us from pursuing a greater destiny. Often, once one milestone is accomplished, we begin to relax and become content with where we are. There has to develop on the inside of each of us a deep hunger to constantly have the appetite for growth. There is so much more to be attained than where we are. Again, everything should accompany His will and desires, but we know those things are far greater than what our minds could ever imagine. It is His good will that we prosper and continue to excel beyond our limitations.

Life itself can be one of the most unattained components that will literally take us on an unexpected journey full of unanswered questions. The most important concept that I have grown to acquire in my short-lived life as a young adult, is that when you know who has all power, and you allow Him to lead you on this orchestrated walk, then you will save yourself from much stress and worry. It is when we learn to yield our issues over to Him, that we will become more powerful than we could have ever imagined. This fight was not fixed for us to handle life's circumstances on our own, but to rest in safety knowing that we have the best attorney on our side.

There is nothing that compares to knowing that you have someone who has your back and best interest at heart. Having a person who has the power to fix anything that you may be facing, and who cares about what concerns you. I am sure that we have all experienced a time in our lives where we may have felt unimportant or of less value to someone who may not have put forth the effort to be there for us when necessary. Thankfully, while resting in the safety zone, God does not allow us to have those feelings. Often, we may not always understand His methods or His ways but we can always rest assured that He will come through with what we need and most importantly, when we need it.

There has never been a time in my life where He has not shown up with what has been a necessary component of my life. Although, I have had to wait and develop patience and long-suffering while in the pursuit of what He has had alongside for me, He has never failed to show up. Many times, we find ourselves putting so much attention toward the problem, instead of keeping our eyes fixed on the one who can solve the troubling issue. Resting areas, cause for us to alleviate all stress and to know that no matter what may come, where we currently are is a place of sobriety, and peace.

To remain in a place of peace of mind, our surroundings must be clear of jaded individuals. Anyone that is going to cloud our judgment or fill our ears with negative words should be removed.

When we come to our resting place, there will come much affliction based on where we have previously come from. People will be assigned to our lives as distractions and detours to get us frustrated or become weary. Whom much is given, much is also required. That is why it is so important that our circle is accompanied by the right people. Individuals who want to see you win.

Dr. Precilla Belin, is a remarkable Godsend that was strategically placed in my life during this time; she was someone who became an essential tool for my spiritual growth and maturity as I began to embark on foreign territory in ministry. She was my mom's childhood friend. Dr. Belin, or Big Sis as I called her lives in Baltimore, Maryland. Cilla became an influential piece of my life by covering me in prayer and imparting sound doctrine and wisdom. Big Sis would always make a conscious decision to call and speak with me before and after speaking engagements. She would even send a seed offering to help cover my gas when on the road. It wasn't that I needed it, but she wanted to support what God was doing in my life. Above anything, she spoke truths into my life that helped shape my future. It is important that we remain surrounded by people that house the ability to push us into our calling. Cilla did that and more.

My sister Ashley, I could write an entire book on what she has been to my life. Her authenticity and ability to remain focused even when adversity has come her way helped mature me in ways that I could not ever imagine. She was one of the most influential pieces of my circle. Although Ashley is a few years older, married, with children, our process was still the same. Because she was gifted and faced many challenges as a young ambassador as I did, it helped being anchored to her. She was a lifeline. Often, I was empowered by her ability to manage being a wife, mother, working woman, and entrepreneur. She did it with such grace and most importantly she honored God. Ashley helped remind me that although you may be in the midst of chaos, there is always sweet assurance in knowing that the God we serve is greater than the minor battle we may be facing. It's our attitude and how we choose to respond that will deliver us from our circumstances. Her gift is so amazing and gem-like. She is a rare jewel on earth, and I am thankful every day of my life that she and I are connected.

Another key element to my life during this phase was my stepfather's dad. Although he was not my biological grandfather, Paw-Paw Larry was necessary during this season of my life. He was a retired school teacher from the Little Rock School District. One of the most successful, hard-working, and loving man I know. Growing up, he and I did not have the closest relationship like we do now, but I always admired his success from a distance. Paw-Paw was quiet. About six months ago, He wrote me a letter explaining that He had read my book, *"Purpose in Adversity"* and how it inspired him. I literally broke down in tears. Here it was all these years, I was astounded by his accomplishments and successes in life, and he found something that I had accomplished to be a motivation.

Thereafter, our journey of rebuilding our relationship began. Paw-Paw Larry and I grew so close over the course of the next few months. His letters were so inspiring. Above all, in each letter about expressing the true meaning of life, he would always make sure that I remembered to keep Jesus as my center. Before we began this new chapter in our relationship, I had no idea that Paw Paw was spiritual. Actually, I never would have guessed that he was. Growing up, we never talked about religion during the times I visited them in Little Rock. We have never attended a church service together. The saying "don't judge a book by its cover" is so profound.

He had no idea that in the middle of him writing me those letters keeping me encouraged was during a desperate time of survival for me. At the moment he began to write was during one of the most troubling seasons of my life. I was frustrated with the curves of handling being a career professional and having a balanced life when I moved back home. Often, I would question if I was doing what I needed to be doing at my age and if I would ever find peace in where I was currently at. Paw Paw's letters seemed to always be on point with the words of encouragement. They were uplifting and motivating at a desperate time in my life. I am just grateful that God allowed him to resurface and become a prominent component in such a delicate time for me.

My twin sisters, Kaylon and Kyelah were lifelines for me. Although I am 6 years older than them, the wisdom that they possess is unreal. They both always encouraged me or gave the extra push when needed. Being raised by a single mom and having the responsibility of modeling good behavior because they were watching your every move was hard but necessary. Now, at 20 years old, they have made me prouder than I could ever be. Kaylon, the baby of the two is a dancer for Arkansas Tech University. She is studying to be a dental hygienist. She is so focused and determined. I feel as if she matured overnight. One day, she was 15 years old starting her first job as a waitress, and now she is a junior in college, working at the dance studio where she gives private dance lessons to young girls and a full-time college student. Kaylon has always been very quiet but she has so much wisdom. She is an observer. Kay doesn't say much, but she sees everything. She plans to relocate to another university to finish her degree because Arkansas Tech doesn't have her specific major. Her drive is contagious, she has a knack for getting things done. Kaylon has never been a procrastinator and it has helped her become the zealous young woman she is today.

Kyelah, the runner, my future Olympian is on the track and field team at Purdue University. A small town girl, with big city dreams; broke odds and chased her dreams. She is the most ambitious and hardworking person I have ever met. I believe her drive and will to be the best has lit a fire in me during my coaching profession. She attended Highland Community College, in Highland Kansas for her first two years of college where she set 13 school records in women's track and field and was the first female athlete of the year. Her relentlessness was unmatched, which is why she was highly recruited and received another track scholarship to one of the most prestigious universities in the country, Purdue. I watched her compete to the highest degree to be the best of them all. She inspires me. Kyelah's personality is also second to none. Unlike Kaylon, she is very outgoing and outspoken. She did not mature as fast as her twin sister, but there is never a dull moment when she's around. I know my mom is proud that not only did she raise us the way she did, but that we went ahead to further our education. We listened.

Watching those two thrive in the real world has been breathtaking. I have a front row seat in witnessing them both excel in their new line of life while being respected citizens at their schools and it makes me proud. Knowing that I succeeded during my time as a collegiate student-athlete and outstanding student in the classroom but now seeing that they're continuing down the same path just makes life much more meaningful. My mom is still very active in our lives although we are all young adults. She works so hard and supports us as much as she did when we were in high school. I still have no idea how she does it. The grace of God is all I can say.

I'd like to encourage anyone who may think that what's in front of you is too hard to conquer. My siblings and I grew up in a single-parent home. Neither our mom nor dad furthered their education beyond high school. Statistics imply that products from those environments that we were raised in are not supposed to finish college, let alone attend college for that matter. It also states that most females will be on welfare and have at least one child before the age 20. But who says that we have to succumb to what those stereotypes suggests? No one. We don't have to; In fact, we possess the power to set the newest trend and create a new statistic. My sisters and I are trying our best, and I highly suggest that you do the same. It's yours for the taking. I encourage you to finish high school, go to college and receive your degree; whatever you decide after that is up to you, just do yourself a favor and don't give up. Education is one of the most powerful tools an individual can have because no matter what, it cannot be taken away from you.

"Education is the most powerful weapon which you can use to change the world"

–Nelson Mandela

✢ My prayer as you learn to divide your assets from your liabilities

Dear God, you said in your word that two can only walk together if they agree. I thank you because I know that everyone who may be struggling with making this tough decision will find hope in you. Give them the strength to relinquish any unnecessary baggage that may be holding them back. We know and believe that you have the authority to connect us to the right people at the right time. I thank you for each person reading this prayer, that they may find divine connections established by you to help push them to their NEXT. Thank you for the confidence that rests in you and for their ability to move forward with the right people by their side. We ask these things in your Name, Amen.

✓ ENDURING a Tough Loss

"Earth has no sorrow that Heaven cannot heal"

December 4, 2017, I lost one of the most influential pieces of my life. DeCario Martez Walter; a humble, loving, outgoing, and free-spirited vessel left this Earth without a final goodbye. The week before then, I received a phone call from his aunt that I needed to make arrangements to come to Houston, Texas and visit him because he wasn't doing well. One side of my inner being had peace because I had seen him down to this point before; on life support, his kidneys failing and lungs in bad condition and literally, I watched God raise him from his ashes. The other part of my soul heard something different in her voice on the other end of the phone and thought to myself I need to hurry and make my way to Texas.

Prior to this phone call that I received about Cario's health, he and I Face-Timed every single day for two weeks straight. He'd start every morning at 5:00 a.m. by saying "girl wake up". That boy is the only person who had the ability to make me so upset and smile at the same time. Our last conversations were some of the best that we ever had. On Thanksgiving Day, he expressed that he was afraid of what was going to happen to him and that his health hadn't been as bad as it currently was. That bothered me because out of all the million and one times he had been sick, he never expressed any feeling of worry. He would always say that he has faith that God was going to bring him out and that He was going to live to be in my wedding and help babysit whenever I had children. This time was different. I heard the sorrow in his voice. The only thing I could do was offer prayer and a belief system. Before we hung up the phone for the last time that I would ever hear his voice, I told him *"God has never lost a battle"*. He answered, "I know pumpkin, I believe that; I am about to take a nap I will call you when I wake up".

Three days passed and I did not hear from him. I called and called. Left message after message and still no reply. That was when his aunt called and expressed to me the severity of his condition and suggested that I make my way down. I had to coach in a basketball game that Saturday morning, and as soon as it ended, I made my way to Houston, Texas. I drove the entire six hours praying and asking God for a miracle for my brother. Once I made my arrival to the hospital and laid eyes on him lying unresponsive in the hospital bed, I knew that he was tired of fighting. I grabbed his hand and said a prayer "God let your will be done". I made it around 4:00 a.m. and did not sleep one wink. The nurses and doctors periodically checked in on him and kept me posted with the details of his health. It wasn't looking good.

The drive back to Arkansas was the most confusing that I've ever experienced after leaving my brother from the hospital. Out of all the many times I had been there for Cario, this time was like none other. We had a basketball game the following Monday, December 4th. None of my players could understand how I made it back and had the strength to coach them. I concluded in my mind that at the end of the week, I was going back to Houston to be with him until he got better. But God had other plans. It was around 8:00 when I checked my phone and noticed that I had six missed calls. None of the people answered when I tried to reach back out. I finally decided to message JoAnna, DeCario's cousin and asked her if she heard anything. She replied back, "*Cario passed away Shanae*". My heart became numb and I lost all feeling. Tears wouldn't flow but my heart was aching.

That was the toughest news that I had ever received in my life. Losing my brother was hard. Burying him was even harder. But honestly, the most difficult part of this process is moving on without him. No more "heart to heart" conversations or early morning laughs. I had to accept that I could no longer get those "big brother" pep talks. Cario helped me gain so much confidence in myself. He would always reassure me that I was beautiful and a rare gem on Earth. He was my protector and I loved him so much for always being so supportive of anything that I wanted to pursue. He will forever be missed, but the love that I have for him will remain the same. He was perfect.

Shanae B. Govan

✝ *My prayer for each of you in transition of enduring a tough loss*

Dear Heavenly Father,

We know that there is no hurt that Heaven cannot heal. I pray that you mend the broken heart of anyone who may be struggling with dealing with a tough loss. I ask that you guide their thoughts and give them peace that surpasses all understanding as you said that you would in your word. God, I ask in your Name that if there is anyone who may be battling with moving forward with their life because of a tough loss, that you fill that empty space that has been left through the passing of their loved one. We know you to be perfect and complete in all things. I thank you because I know that they will find hope, love, and rest in you during this hard time. In your name I pray, Amen.

✓ *Transitioning in Your NOW*

"Opportunity often comes disguised in the form of misfortune, or temporary defeat"

-Napoleon Hill

I have made countless mistakes at this point in my life. I have unintentionally taken the wrong advice. Hurt people. I have abused friendships. There have been episodes of repeated cycles of growth because of going back to what was "familiar". I have even settled in areas of my maturing phase to become better. Experienced many failed attempts at life. There have been setbacks and disappointments caused by the actions of my decisions. I have literally during this anticipated place, discovered that my flaws make me who I am. The bittersweet part of embracing my NOW is knowing that none of those things define me, but instead they push me to a greater place in growth and most importantly in God.

We should realize that our future is unborn and waiting for us to come forth with open arms. It will take care of itself. That is why it is very important to rest in our NOW and prepare for where we are headed. I have learned that if you get ready NOW, then once you arrive at the destination of your NEXT, you won't have to prepare then, because you will be in position for what has need of you. It is important that we keep this in perspective and allow our minds to remain fixed on living in the MOMENT of our current situation.

Shanae B. Govan

I am so thankful that God had prepared my feet for where they currently are. Coming back home to coach was attached to several components that had nothing to do with basketball. So much adversity was connected to this seat; it was hard but worth it. Moving to Crossett, I knew that I was going to be surrounded by a lot of individuals who wanted the community to change and go in another direction. I had positive influences in my corner that always seemingly had something good to say. But this process wasn't going to happen overnight.

Our black community was beginning to piece itself back together. I believe it had a lot to do with me making the decision to commit to moving back and what it meant for our culture. Because the last African American female coach that we had previously at Crossett High was my Godmother, and mentor coach Lucy Williams who had been gone for over ten years at this point. Now, to have someone like me to be the face of the program was a proud moment for our African American community. It brought hope. Most importantly, it allowed our young people to see that we could make a change. We had the power to hold professional positions within the school district and be fairly young while doing it. It modeled the possibility that we possessed the power to be anything that we pursued. Our race did not have to succumb to the negative stereotypes often attached. Every day for those kids and our community, I wasn't just "Coach G" but I symbolized *"Change, Hope, and Pride"* for my people.

The first year of coaching was tough, but rewarding also. My senior high basketball team did not do as well as I expected coming in. Most of the people who saw the girls prior to my return would constantly keep me encouraged while reminding us that building a program takes time. They were right. But you had a few, who had negative things to say no matter what. Our efforts were never enough. The most frustrating part for me was having the desire for that process to go a little quicker than it had been going for us. We weathered the storm of adversity and got better day by day. I never gave up or felt defeated because of the journey.

We accomplished something that hadn't been done in a while which was winning the first game of the district tournament. We had been seeded 4th in our conference which was last place and had to play the third place team on the north side. The team was DeWitt. They had a better season than what we had, but I felt that we were at the point where we had nothing to lose. Because our junior high season had ended a week before, I could move up my two best players to contend with us in our district tournament. Jada and Anaya had a great work ethic and would do whatever I asked of them. Before the game, I told them both to just go out and have fun if their name was called to enter the game. Not only did those two have fun while playing in their first high school game, but they both were our overall leading scorers in our victory. They made me proud. I was thankful that we were able to win that game for the seniors. They needed that experience because since they were in the 7th grade, they have not had any success; but this moment changed that for them in closing of their basketball careers. I embraced it all.

In closing of our season, I had a group that was a bright spot and represented what our future would mirror. The Junior Lady Eagles did something that had not been done since 1992, the year I was born. These ambitious, hard-working, relentless players tied for first place in our conference with a record of 5-2 and an overall record of 12-6. It is my desire to leave my legacy at Crossett. Those girls accomplished something that my teammates did not achieve when I attended the junior high school 11 years ago as a ninth grader, and that's winning a championship title.

There were a few times where I allowed some losses with the senior girls and some moments of confusion to overwhelm and cloud my judgment. In everything, when God has placed you in a position to be a trailblazer, you must be willing to accept that everyone will not like you, they will not support you, and it has nothing to do with you, but everything to do with what is on the inside. I had a few of those people assigned to my journey in Crossett. It made me tough and helped develop another level of humility.

There were some parents who were upset that I did not play their daughter that much, in exchange for their displeasure of the way I ran my program; they did things to sabotage my name in order for others to dislike me. That comes with the territory. I had to understand everyone was not going to be pleased with my decisions. If you desire to be a coach, and you're concerned about pleasing people, then you need to choose another profession.

Some people talked about how I dressed for ball games because I chose to wear high heels, and dress professionally.

Individuals would suggest that I was "out-dressing" my team, or that I was "over" dressed, or "doing too much" with wearing heels with professional attire. Why what I chose to wear for our games mattered so much I am not sure, but I do know it impacted my girls. They'd always compliment me and some would even say they wanted to be like me when they grow up. I knew that for some of those girls, I was the only positive influence they had in their life. The one person they've had in their close circle who modeled how a young woman should carry herself modestly. It was about showing some of my players who needed guidance in that area that women can be classy and respectable at the same time. We don't have to wear skin tight clothes or show cleavage to get attention. I wanted to express to them through the way I dressed that presentation is everything. I also knew that one day I would be a college coach, and they all dress like that. I was in preparation for my NEXT.

    I gained the understanding that no matter what I wore, something would be said in both perspectives. Some people would like what I wore, and some would not. If I chose to wear sweatpants or khakis, things would still be speculated.

Nevertheless, I realized that the choices I made did not affect those who formed an opinion. The reflection of who I presented to be had nothing to do with those individuals, but it was about myself and my program. Professionalism is what I desired to represent, and that's what I did. My players embraced it. So despite the ignorant and close-minded statements of people looking to spread negativity, I refused to lower my standards. At the end of the day, when I prepared for games, I did not consider what fans or critics would think. I was dressing for where I was headed, not for where my feet were planted at the moment. In all those circumstances, and several others that are not worth discussing, I had to realize that it was bigger than me. Nevertheless, I couldn't take what they said personal or to heart because if so, then they'd win. I was bigger than that, mentally and emotionally.

Although I knew those things, I could not treat those individuals any less than how human beings deserve to be handled. That was my rightful duty as a change agent but most importantly in my walk as a Christian. Anytime someone is coming in and rebuilding, it is evident that everyone cannot handle it; especially when they are not included in the process. Of those times that I did become discouraged or questioned why I was rerouted to my hometown to hear the negative comments, God reminded me that it was for His glory. I could not take any of it personal. We take on battles that were not intended for us to fight. That was God's mission; He just allowed me to be a resource that he used during the journey. As a result, every decision I made was important for me to realize that I represented Him. My actions, reactions, responses, and ability to treat others in a respectable manner reflected who He was in my life.

When those thoughts flooded my heart, I remembered the times students would reach out and express that I was their role model. Every class period, young boys and girls would come to my room in between breaks to just speak or sit and talk. Most of these students, I did not teach and weren't on my basketball team. Students like Jabari, Kyler, Derrick, and Man loved to talk about sports and what they could do to get better; that made me feel special since they thought enough of me as a female coach that I could help improve their skills because of the impact I had on my team. My faithful players, India, Haleigh, Quintavia, Jada, Te'A, Glinda, and Jaylynn never missed a period without stopping by to say hello. Davonne, also a unique individual became one of my mentees. He is someone who will do great things in life because of his ambition and drive to be great. That symbolized being a positive influence on the student body. The one time my player Endia wrote her essay on my book and said it inspired her, made me feel loved and appreciated. There was also a time when I ran into one of the school board members from Hamburg in Wal-Mart and he told me that he hated the day that they let me go because their basketball program and entire school needed a Shanae Govan desperately. It was a breathtaking and monumental moment for me.

Those things kept me grounded along with having my mentors Coach Robert and Lucy Williams along with a host of others who I knew were covering me in prayer and friends who believed in me regardless of what was said negatively about the movement that was taking place through the works of my hands. My former 8th-grade basketball coach, Dannisha (Armstrong) Stroud was always supportive of me although it had been over ten years since she coached me in junior high; she still had a crucial impact on my life. Her support meant everything to me. She was someone I always aspired to be like because of her passion for us even as a coach and also a mentor. Her words of motivation and encouragement even during my young adult life as a coach helped me on some of the tough days that I questioned if I was in the right profession. I was thankful to God for surrounding me with ambassadors and successful coaches as these were.

If we want success, we must realize that it will come with a lot more than just a title. There is an expensive grind to this process. Everyone sees the Hollywood-like portion, but no one wants all that transpires behind the scenes. The things that take place when no one is looking are what make us who we are. The late night work hours when you are off the clock, are adjacent to being great. The disrespect of being judged because you choose to take a different route than what has previously been taken by others who were in your position, or who wished they had the opportunity, adds a greater sense of stability that allows you to grow in more ways than ever imagined.

Coaching has to be one of the toughest careers to pursue. In this seat, we as head coaches put our fate in the hands of teenage kids. We all know what it is like to be a teen. We are spoiled, entitled, emotional, hard-headed, stubborn, and selfish. I loved every bit of my job, having the opportunity to mold and shape my girls to be better not just on the court, but in life. They drove me crazy with their inconsistencies, but we were all growing through the many maturing pains. I evolved and so did they. It was beautiful. What I was dealing with was more than what people on the outside could see. My job was consumed with having to teach girls how to be young women. It was more than just drawing up plays or blowing a whistle. I had to show these ladies that in order for us to be successful, we had to abandon our egos and attitudes; starting with myself. I wouldn't trade it for anything. The best thing to ever happen to me besides accepting Jesus Christ was deciding to be a head girls' basketball coach.

Those young frail tadpoles would one day be relentless, courageous, ambassadors leading companies to the road towards success. I embraced knowing that I was their mirror for change. I even became a portion of their hope and future. So, with every bit of adversity and turmoil attached to being back, I took it. It was necessary and a part of where God was taking me. He was preparing me for my NEXT. This process could not be rushed. I lived in my NOW because I knew that my latter would be greater than my former. My *destiny* was not attached to this job; it was just a stepping stone to get to the next place.

When you are in a profession and forced to deal with people, it is important that you do not allow the affairs of life or the hardship of dealing with difficult individuals deter you from the assignment. It is all part of the necessary process and components that will help push you to the desired place of growth. Those elements are needed. They help mature us in a way that nothing else has the ability to do so. Honestly, it never has anything to do with you as a person, but it is all connected to the assignment.

Overall, I loved being back home in Crossett. I had more people for me than were against me. Of those few that were not on board with the shift, I can honestly say that God connected me to some of the most prominent forces in our small town. There were Pastors and great leaders in our community that stood with me. They realized the weight of having me back home and in our schools. The wanted to help pour into my ministry. This went beyond basketball, but this seat was connected to my *destiny*. Often, we allow those small affairs such as who doesn't like us to distract and offset our focus. It magnifies the situation and makes it bigger than what it truly is in essence.

It's important that we do not get upset when there's a detour on the way to our **destiny**. We have to keep a good attitude and trust that it is all for the making of who we are becoming. There is only so much emotional energy that we can exert each day. There is no need in fighting battles that don't matter. Every test in our life has the opportunity to make us either bitter or better and every problem that arises appears to break us or make us. We have to train our minds to be calm in every situation; especially those that we have no control over. When you blame others for your adversities, you give them the power to stop the evolution of your maturing phases; we must shift our focus and trust God.

The **gateway to destiny** is sometimes a hard path. I was so thankful that down this journey, God even puts an influential person in my life that was well-known not only in our town or state but across our nation. Mrs. Toyce Newton, founder of the Phoenix Youth Services in Crossett, became my mentor. This was probably one of the most humbling experiences that I had received while being back. She and her staff worked together to aid at-risk youth in our community while helping bridge the gap between students and success.

Not everyone can say that they graduated college, moved off and began their career, and then decided to come back HOME. That decision had nothing to do with me. Because honestly, had I been able to do what I wanted to do initially, I would have been in Clarksville, Tennessee working under my former head basketball coach David Midlick whom I played for at Delta State. He was now in his third season at the D1 collegiate basketball program Austin Peay University and had room for me be a member of his staff. God saw differently. It has never been a dream of mine to coach on the college level, but having the chance to serve under the man who made me the coach that I am today, was an opportunity of a lifetime. When I called and told him the news of accepting the job in Crossett and not being one of his staff at Austin Peay, he was elated. Coach Mid always supported any decision of mine especially when it revolved around making myself a better professional.

Our NOW moments are sent to equip us for the ongoing journey that lies ahead. There is no need in outrunning or having the desire to get beyond the current moment before it is time. The safest place to be is in the will of God. That is where I found myself at this moment of my life. People told me that I was crazy for moving back home and taking that job especially with the dynamics of the girls' basketball program being as poor as it was and considering how far I had come at my previous school in MS. The year I left those girls, was the year that we were supposed to be one of the top teams in the conference. My mentor, Coach Lucy Williams once told me, to always leave a program better than the way you found it, and that is what I did. Transitioning back to my hometown was exciting because I had the opportunity to change mindsets and give back to a dying community through a platform that I have embraced for most of my young adult life; loving the game of basketball while teaching kids to embrace the adversities of life. What better way than to do it in the city where you found your purpose and that watered the many seeds that were planted in your life?

A deep revelation appeared to me while journeying through this process. Had I not embraced being in Mississippi those long, sometimes aggravating, temperament teaching years of growth, then I would have not been prepared for where my feet are currently positioned now. Each level of the developmental process that we transition through has the same method of teaching attached to it. The sum of the components of growth is that every lesson is connected to your NEXT. We have one or two choices; either we mentally and wholeheartedly commit to the shift or we can sit in a corner and die internally. It is uncomfortable. But it brings out the best in us.

Challenges continuously attacked my thought process to check my focus. I had to starve my fears and doubts and feed those negative thoughts with the truth; God's truth. Some of my friends were at this point in our lives, getting married. A few of them were going through divorces. This chapter of their lives even allowed them to become parents. That was not the case for me. I was single and had no children. People would often ask, "What are you waiting on" or "so and so is married and you're 26 you need to hurry and find a man". I had to remind them that I was running MY course. When God was ready, He would send the one to find me. It was not time for those things yet in my life. I had to commit to not allowing people to push me to a place of rushing my growth process. Because where I was in my life I did not have time for a committed relationship or for children. My feet were planted back home to administer truth to the many lives that were attached to my hands.

If you have yet to discover your purpose in life, that is just fine. Do not allow individuals to rush that process of evolution for you. That is your race and your journey. It belongs to YOU. Commit to embodying that concept of growth in divorcing yourself from the opinions of others. Critical people always will find a way to force you into or out of something but most of those individuals have a hard time seeing themselves through that same scope of criticism as they're projecting towards others. OWN where you are, and EMBRACE where you are headed without the help of people who are not committed to understanding your process.

The transition of gravitating to your anticipated SEAT here on earth has a way of pushing us to crave change. It is with great hope and promise that each of you, as you grow in wholeness and sobriety that you honor where you are NOW. We cannot go back and change what has transpired in our past, but we can do something about what is in our midst. I challenge each of you that are reading this, to allow DESTINY to be awakened on the inside of you. Truth being told, we have all settled enough in our lives and have at some point accepted being average. If we are going to press beyond all limitations, setbacks, and disappointments, then we must first abandon that way of processing. I believe that God allowed us all to go through these adversities only to put us on the path to something GREAT. Whether your good outweighs your bad, or vice versa, know that it won't always be like this. I encourage each of you, to position yourself to embrace where you are, and press toward your higher calling which is in Christ Jesus. YOUR DESTINY AWAITS YOUR ARRIVAL!!!

✝ *My prayer for the TRANSITION in Your NOW.*

Dear God, I pray that as each of your people begin to embark on foreign territory that they yield their hearts to the promises that you have given them. I pray that during this phase of arriving at their destination that nothing shakes their belief in who you are. I stand in the gap for them believing that they will have hope and strength to embody where they are NOW while in transition to their new beginning. Guide their feet and hands. I pray that these believers remain in your perfected will while trusting the strategies that you use to prepare them for this new season in life. Allow their hearts to remain anchored and abide by your desires while abandoning their own. I thank you in advance for granting every petition that your believers have set aside for you. Amen.

Remember, this journey that we are on is bigger than where we are now. I want to encourage and strengthen you to remain in the fight. It will be worth it in the end. Stay the course and know that God has not forgotten about you. Your future is bright!

-Awaken to your Destiny

Shanae B. Govan

I would like to dedicate this last chapter of "The Destination" to 44 uniquely crafted young women who have played a significant role in helping shape and mold me to be the professional, coach, and mentor that I am today. It is with great hope and high expectation that they use the tools that were given to them through our years together at Crossett to become ambassadors within the society. These young women will be your future leaders of America and whatever their hands touch will prosper.

Love Always,
Coach G

Ali Rindt	Lydia Burnett	Quintavia Simpson	Martasia Smith
	Brooke Courson	Shekirra Gavin	Endia Jenkins
	Reshenna DeFord	Treasure Ellis	Haleigh Boston
	Jenna Cate Robert	Nakydra Paskel	Nakari Thrower
	Jaquesha Brown	Niya Jackson	Allie Thurmon
	Tramesha Lewis	Jayden Thurmon	Makayla Foster
Lana Carter	Sunni Lee	Jaylynn Hampton	Harmony Green
Milli Vargas	Adrienne Spencer	Glinda Clark	Abby Senn
Angel Smith	Charity Watkins	Jada Cooks	LaStar Thompson
	Kirsten Thurman	Te'A Jenkins	Charla Montgomery
	Kristen Parks	Heavenly McDade	Hannah Govan
Anaya Jones	Gracie Lane	Chloe Monroe	Jazmine Hendrix
	Tkia Montgomery	Lyndsee Watt	Jasmine Fletcher

Interested in Writing and or Publishing a BOOK???

Visit: www.A2ZBooksPublishing.net

www.ingramcontent.com/pod-product-compliance
Lightning Source LLC
Chambersburg PA
CBHW070108120526
44588CB00032B/1379